T0249270

Alex Macl

SCHOOL PLAY

OBERON BOOKS
LONDON

WWW.OBERONBOOKS.COM

First published in 2017 by Oberon Books Ltd
521 Caledonian Road, London N7 9RH
Tel: +44 (0) 20 7607 3637 / Fax: +44 (0) 20 7607 3629
e-mail: info@oberonbooks.com
www.oberonbooks.com

A catalogue record for this book is available from the British Library.

PB ISBN: 9781786821232
E ISBN: 9781786821249

Cover: Photograph by AP; Image Design by Atri Banerjee

In memory of my Grandad.

Characters

LARA
Headteacher's administrative assistant at St
Barnabas' Primary School (mid 20s).

JO
Headteacher of St Barnabas' Primary School
(late 40s/early 50s).

TOM
A private tutor on a placement at the school
(early 20s).

TONY
The school caretaker (40s).

DAVID
The father of Hannah, a Year 6 pupil
(mid 30s-40s).

MIKAELA/MIKEL
A pupil at the school (10-12).*

*This part can be played by a male or female actor.

Note

[ ] indicates an unspoken train of thought.

/ indicates an overlap with the following line of speech.

– mid-speech indicates the speaker's own interjection; at the end of a line marks an interruption by another speaker.

… mid-speech indicates a hesitation; at the end of a line of speech indicates a trailing off; as stand-alone dialogue this indicates a reluctance to speak or struggle to formulate a response.

Act 1

July, 2017.

The double office in a primary school in South West London, partitioned by a thin wall.

The inner portion of the room belongs to the headteacher. On a desk, among the detritus of a busy office, is a bloods kit for diabetes. There is a huge revolving whiteboard filled with information: the nerve centre of the school.

The ante-office is that of the administrative assistant. There is a desk, a sofa, two small classroom chairs, a low table with a kettle, a box of teabags, instant coffee and four mugs. Large filing cabinets dot the room. Behind the desk hangs a smaller whiteboard filled with appointments. A door gives onto the corridor.

Fluorescent strip lights hang in the office and the corridor outside. We get the impression that this is an arena of controlled chaos.

Silence. A clock hanging on the wall reads 7.30am. The door is closed. The fluorescents light up. One of them flickers sporadically, then resumes a steady glow.

Footsteps along the outer corridor approach. A couple of soft exhalations, the sound of struggling with a trivial but difficult task. The door handle moves slowly down once, then flicks back up. A shuffling. The door handle moves down again, flicks back again.

LARA: *(Softly.)* Fuck it.

More shuffling, the hollow clink of tin on stone. The door swings slowly open. Behind it LARA Hudson, the headteacher's administrative assistant, is crouching to pick up a can of Diet Coke off the floor, groping as if she can't quite see it. She is mid-twenties, tired as hell, and hungover. She carries a handbag, a lever-arch file and a stack of post. She picks up the can and walks behind the desk. Behind her, through the door, a large Year 2 display is partially visible.

LARA dumps the arch file down onto her desk, throws the post on top of it, letting the handbag slip from her arm. Opening one drawer after another she rifles around the desk until she finds a pair of glasses and puts them on with relief, a minor exhalation of 'yes', blinking and adjusting her eyes to lenses which aren't quite her prescription any more. She grabs a silver packet of Ibuprofen from an open drawer and drinks two tablets with the coke.

She checks the clock, looks for a place to set her drink, settling on a position just in front of the keyboard. She boots up the computer, which makes the Windows welcome noise.

LARA: *(Turning to the post.)* Ok...

She begins to look through the post, throwing some letters into her box, setting others aside. She hums to herself. She reaches the penultimate letter, a brown A4 envelope, and pauses over it. She checks the date.

She turns back to the post, sets the other letter in her own box and begins to open the brown envelope with a finger, working feverishly, checking the corridor. She stops, takes the second pile and the envelope, walks into the larger office, places them in the postbox on the desk. As she turns away she remembers something, consults her phone and goes to the whiteboard. She changes the time on a note: 'L.A. Meeting: 10am' becomes 'L.A. Meeting: 11.30am.' Spotting the Natural History Museum notice on the whiteboard, she doodles a dinosaur, complete with feathers, below it.

As she turns she eyes the envelope again, grapples with temptation, and decides to open it. She grabs a letter opener on the desk, sets about her task, and stops again, throwing the letter in its box and setting the opener back in frustration. She returns to the smaller office, turns the kettle on, settles back to her own desk, opens up the lever arch files, withdraws an A4 sheet from a plastic wallet along with a pile of cheques and permission slips, and begins to tick names on the sheet with a red biro. She checks the computer screen, scribbles a new post-it note.

LARA eyes the kettle as it comes to the boil, checks the clock, stands up suddenly. She darts to the larger office, takes the brown envelope again. She hurries to the kettle, holds the envelope over the steam. She checks the clock, inspects the seal of the envelope. She has forgotten the opener.

She reaches across to the desk, stretching out for the biro while keeping the envelope over the steam. She brings the biro back and begins to slide it under the seal when she hears footsteps on the corridor. As the footsteps draw nearer, she glides across to the larger office. She presses the envelope closed again, places it in the middle of the pile of post in the box, smoothes her shirt and walks back into her own office. The door opens.

LARA: Morning, Jo.

JO Fell enters. She carries a large satchel, wears a suit, and is overworked. There is a newspaper under her arm. She doesn't stop in LARA'S office, but keeps moving until she gets to her own desk.

JO: Hi, Lara.

LARA: How are you?

JO: You know, fine. Good evening?

LARA: Hm?

JO: Did you have a good evening? Last night?

LARA: Yeah. Well, no, I just stayed late here, but… Yeah. You?

JO: School night.

JO reaches her desk, hesitates over the kit bag, picks it up.

JO: *(Almost a question.)* No one picked up the bloods kit.

LARA: Sorry?

JO: The insulin. Did nobody come for it yesterday?

LARA: All quiet after you left. That one's ours, isn't it?

JO: Ours is in the sick bay.

LARA: I can check with reception –

JO: It's fine, I'll keep it here.

LARA: Whose is it?

JO: It's for a parent. Don't worry, I'll sort it.

JO looks at the pile of post.

JO: God, that's a lot of post.

LARA: *(Shiftily.)* Yeah.

JO: *(Looking to the board.)* Week and a half to go.

JO walks into LARA's office.

LARA: I haven't had a chance to go through them all yet but / I think –

JO: Could I get a coffee, Lara – oh. Glasses.

LARA: What? Oh, yeah.

JO: Haven't seen you in glasses for years.

LARA: They're different glasses.

JO: I know.

LARA: Prescription changed.

JO: And your head's grown.

LARA: Yeah.

JO: Not like that.

LARA: No. Well. No. *(Beat.)* Just thought I'd give my eyes a break.

JO: Sure. Could I get a coffee?

LARA: Yes.

During the following LARA makes two coffees, as JO surveys the whiteboard in her office.

JO: How's your dad?

LARA: He's fine. Managing. I missed him yesterday.

JO: Not because of work?

LARA: No.

JO: You know, if you ever have to leave / early…

LARA: He just goes to bed earlier these days.

JO: Sure. Let me know when I can pop round.

LARA: Yeah I will, he'd love to see you. Just need to make sure the nurse isn't in.

JO: I don't mind.

LARA: He does. *(Half-beat.)* I'm keeping him updated.

JO: On?

LARA: Everything here. He misses it.

JO: He's still got the governors' meetings.

LARA: But it's not the same. He loves the gossip.

JO: I remember. *(Beat.)* They're cooler, by the way.

LARA: Sorry?

JO: Those glasses. Cooler than the ones you had before.

LARA: The ones with Barbie on the frames?

JO: Yeah.

LARA: Yeah, it was time to move on.

> *Beat.*

JO: Ok, so, today.

> *This routine is run every day. It is more tense than usual today. LARA consults post-its, her computer, phone and mini-whiteboard.*

LARA: So: James emailed, the Local Authority have pushed back your meeting to eleven thirty.

JO: What? Why?

LARA: He didn't say.

JO: Jesus. When did he email?

LARA: Quarter to seven.

JO: I can't make eleven thirty.

LARA: Actually you can, I emailed Sue Finning and she's happy to meet you at 10.

JO: When did you sort that?

LARA: Ten to seven.

JO: Early.

LARA: I was up.

JO: So was I. *(Beat.)* Why are they pushing it back?

LARA: He didn't say.

JO: Power brunch?

LARA: I don't think they do those.

JO: An extra hour and a half to 'improve,' I suppose.

LARA: I'm sure it's nothing.

Beat.

JO: Sue wants to talk about after school club, doesn't she?

LARA: Yep.

JO: Not breakfast club.

LARA: I don't think so.

JO: Is that on the board?

LARA: Yeah, it should be.

JO: Great. Which one?

LARA: *(Knowing she means 'which kids'.)* She wants Luke to stop activities because he's joining the cubs.

JO: *(Remembering.)* Right.

LARA: But she's keeping Miriam and Phoebe in.

JO: Yes.

LARA: And all three are going to carry on with breakfast club.

JO: Yep, I remember now.

LARA: Frank Wallis has emailed asking to take Saul and Petra out for the last week of term.

JO: Where?

LARA: You're not gonna like this.

JO: Go on.

LARA: Spain.

JO: Spain?

LARA: Spain.

JO: Lovely. Forward that on to Social Welfare.

LARA: Sure.

JO: I don't know why he's bothered emailing.

LARA: Maybe he wants people to know he's going to Spain.

JO: Maybe. What else?

LARA: Tony wants to talk to you about the playground.

JO: What about the playground?

LARA: The asphalt by the gates is coming apart, he said some parents have been complaining.

JO: To whom?

LARA: To him. In person, nothing written.

JO: So he wants to re-lay it?

LARA: Yeah, I think so.

JO: Right. I haven't noticed.

LARA: But if he's getting complaints… And we've got the holidays coming up, so.

JO: *(Snapping.)* It's not the time, it's the money. *(Beat.)* I can see him at two for half an hour.

LARA: *(Scribbling a post-it.)* I'll let him know.

JO: And tell him to draw up a budget, if he can. Just preliminary stuff.

JO writes up the meeting on the board.

LARA: Sure.

The fluorescent light flickers.

LARA: Do you mind if I ask him to have a look at that fluoro as well?

JO: *(Looking up at it.)* Oh, yeah. Sure.

LARA: It's been doing it for ages.

JO studies the light. LARA has made the coffees, carries one mug through to JO's office and places it on her desk.

JO: *(Off the board.)* All the home school workers are in today… Jan wanted to have a word about Michael, didn't she?

LARA: Pencilled that in at 2.40.

JO: Won't that be in the middle of a session?

LARA: That's when his session starts.

JO: *(Seeing the logic.)* So we can talk to him together, fine.

13

She scribbles up the meeting, consults the timetable affixed to the top of the board.

JO: And I can drop into Year 3's reading group after that, perfect. You remember Biff, Chip and Kipper, don't you?

LARA: Yeah, we read those with you. You did the voices.

JO: Still do.

LARA: Oh. Great. I'll let Carolyn know you're coming.

JO: No, I'll surprise them.

LARA: Ok.

JO: And Year 6 have got their trip.

LARA: Yeah, I got an email from the museum, both workshops are booked.

JO: Which are they doing?

LARA: Uh, fun with fossils –

JO: Of course.

LARA: And the dino scene investigation.

JO: Sounds forensic. *(Gesturing to the board.)* I like the T-Rex.

LARA: Velociraptor.

JO: Oh.

LARA: 'Cause it's got the feathers, look.

JO: Wait – velociraptors had feathers?

LARA: Yeah. They found out recently.

JO: We've all been lied to.

LARA: I've got the codes of conduct ready to print. But some permission slips haven't come through.

JO: Oh. *(Masking concern.)* Which ones?

LARA: James Fielker, Hannah Martin and Zan Rashid.

JO: I spoke to James' mum yesterday and I know Zan is bringing his today.

LARA: *(Scratching these off a post-it note.)* What about Hannah?

JO: I'll see if her mum has it – no, it's her dad today. Coach leaves after assembly, he's got time.

LARA: They know about the cheques?

JO: We've got Hannah's cheque.

LARA: The others, though.

JO: We sent out letters at the start of term.

LARA: I know, / but –

JO: Don't worry about the cheques. It's the permission slips. *(Half-beat.)* We'll get them. Anything else?

LARA: Tom's in for Year Six tutoring.

JO: But they've got the trip.

LARA: After the trip.

JO: Did we sign off on that?

LARA: He's contracted to three more sessions.

JO: Seems a bit harsh to bring them back for a lesson.

LARA: It had to be today, really.

   Pause.

LARA: He's quite creative. I mean, trying to make it more collaborative.

JO: *(Dismissive.)* The Montessori Method?

LARA: I think it's quite interesting, organized play…

JO: Have you seen any of his lessons?

LARA: No. Just talked about it.

JO: Ah, right.

LARA: Once or twice, you know, when he's been in.

JO: Well, so long as TruThought get their commission.

LARA: It's changing its name.

JO: The tutoring agency?

LARA: Yeah, got an email yesterday.

JO: To what?

LARA: FreeMind Tutors.

JO: That sounds like a cult.

LARA: Yeah.

JO: Oh, how are we doing on reports?

LARA: Well, Year 2 and 6 are waiting on the results.

JO: I know, but the others?

LARA: All in apart from Year 5 attendance records.

JO: They've never not been late.

LARA: And on Tom's. But that's through the agency.

JO: Ok, can we chase those up?

LARA: Yep, I'll email TruThought today.

JO: No, the attendance records, that's the priority. I don't care about Tom's.

LARA: Yep, I'll get onto Year 5.

JO: Leave the agency for now. SuperBrains or MindFart or whatever they're called.

LARA: Sure. And tomorrow / you've got –

JO: I can't do tomorrow today. *(Turning from the whiteboard.)* We'll jump off that bridge when we get to it.

LARA: Sure. We'll do tomorrow tomorrow.

JO boots up her computer. LARA's phone rings. She picks it up.

LARA: Hello, St Barnabas'... Hi Angela... Well, thank you... Yep, sure, that's no problem... She can wait here... I know she is... No, of course. Thanks for letting me know... You too, bye.

She puts the phone down and begins to scribble a post-it note.

LARA: Jo, it's alright if Mikaela stays here for fifteen minutes after home-time? Angela's shift just came through.

JO: That's fine. She's well-behaved.

LARA: That's what I said.

LARA scribbles on the post-it note.

JO: Right, post.

LARA: Yeah, I was going to say, I think one of them might be
the results.

JO: The SATs?

LARA: Yeah. It's the fifth.

Beat.

JO: Yeah.

JO looks at her watch, glances at the mailbox.

JO: Which one?

LARA: The brown one, I think.

JO: Aha.

She takes the envelope out from the pile, inspects it.

JO: The one you've tried to open?

LARA: Yeah.

Beat.

JO: Repeatedly?

LARA: Yeah.

JO: Have you seen them?

LARA: No. You interrupted me. I'm really sorry.

JO: Don't be.

LARA: I wasn't trying to–

JO: Honestly, it's fine.

*JO stands holding the results. She can't open them. Sounds of the
playground begin to surface as parents and pupils arrive.*

JO: Can I get another coffee?

LARA: I put it on your desk.

Beat.

LARA: They're going to be the same whether you open them
now –

JO: I know.

LARA: – or in fifteen minutes.

JO: I know.

Beat.

LARA: And they don't change anything. *(Off Jo's look.)* It doesn't change them.

JO: No.

LARA: Those are just numbers.

JO: *(Sharply.)* Is that what they tell you in teacher training?

LARA: No. *(Half-beat.)* The awards are important, but they're / not –

JO: Not what I'm worried about.

LARA: Exactly. If we can go in for them, great, but they're a bonus.

JO: Yeah. *(Half-beat.)* That's how to think about it.

LARA: There's no guarantee we'd win one.

JO: There's a chance.

LARA: Right.

Silence. JO opens the envelope, looks at the header on the first page.

LARA: It's definitely them?

JO: It's them, yeah.

Long beat.

LARA: Do you want me / to [take a look?]

JO: Would you close the door, Lara?

LARA: *(Glancing towards the corridor.)* It's already closed.

JO: This door. *(She gestures to the door of the dividing wall.)* Just for a minute.

LARA: 'Course.

LARA closes the door. JO sits down, toys with the envelope. She opens it and withdraws several sheets. She reads through the first page, then scans through the rest. She reads over it again. And again. When she can't look at the numbers anymore, she slowly puts the paper down. She breathes deeply, is still. She looks down. We understand bad news.

JO: *(Quietly.)* Damn.

She presses a button on the phone. A beep.

VOICEMAIL: Hi Jo, it's James, just hoping you got the message about the new time for today's meeting, we've just had to push it back slightly. I spoke to your secretary but just in case –

JO deletes the message. A beep. The next message emits, a new voice.

VOICEMAIL: Morning, Jo, it's Sarah, hope all's well, just wanted to say the emails from the Schools' Department at the Museum are only coming through to me now, just thought that would be easier. But I'm going to forward them to you just for the records – I'm sure I'll see you and let you know in person, but just in case I don't I thought I'd leave this so you're not wondering why you're not getting any emails from them. Sorry this is very long. See you later, bye.

JO shakes her head, deletes the message. A beep. Next message. Another voice.

VOICEMAIL: Hello, only me.

JO stops.

VOICEMAIL: I can't get through on the mobile so I thought I'd try you here, you must, um – not be in yet. I know it's not ideal, but you're not picking up at home either, so… Yep. Just checking you were all set for tomorrow, might be nice to talk to you without the solicitor. I found the ma –

Suddenly her hand darts to the phone, lifting up and replacing the receiver. The message cuts out. With a sharp intake of breath she sits up, folds the paper into the envelope and turns to the desktop. LARA approaches JO's door.

LARA: Jo?

JO: Come in.

LARA: How did we do?

JO: Compared to last year?

LARA: Um, yeah?

JO: Hard to tell exactly. It's the new scaled scores, so we can't compare. We're not meant to, apparently.

LARA: Can go for the awards?

JO hesitates.

JO: I'll have to have a staff meeting before we apply, just to discuss the results.

LARA: I can book that in.

JO: And one with the governors.

LARA: I'll do that for you.

JO: It doesn't have to / be [right now].

LARA: But we're eligible, aren't we? They make us eligible.

JO: We could be eligible.

LARA: So you'll apply for it.

JO: *(Firmly.)* It doesn't work like that. I've got to run it through the right channels. Just to make sure we've got the basis for an application.

LARA: I thought we qualified just by having kids on the pupil premium? If the marks are / high enough…

JO: This is a new system, so it depends on results at other schools / as well –

LARA: Don't the scaled scores do that already?

JO: *(Ending this.)* Let's schedule a staff meeting later today.

LARA: *(Checked.)* Sure.

JO: Say 3.30? Shouldn't take long.

LARA: I'll send an email round.

LARA returns to her desk as JO goes towards the whiteboard, pen in hand.

JO: And the board of governors… Tomorrow?

LARA: It might be a bit short notice for them.

JO: Friday?

LARA: That's still quite soon. *(Off JO's look.)* I'll find you a time.

JO: Thanks, Lara.

JO writes up her new appointments on the board. She turns back to the results on her desk, takes up the envelope and places it in one of the filing cabinets.

LARA: I can make a copy of those? For the Local Authority.

JO: I shouldn't think they'll need it.

LARA watches her and turns her head away as JO softly closes the cabinet. The fluorescent light flickers. The voices in the playground are rising.

LARA: Sure. I'll nip out and chase up those permission slips.

JO: I'll do it.

LARA: I'm happy to.

JO: No, I'm on duty. *(She picks the blood kit up off the desk, stops at LARA's desk.)* Do you have any spares?

LARA: Yep.

LARA hands JO a few permission slips.

JO: Thanks. Let me know what time you think'll work for the governors.

LARA: Will do. Sorry, I didn't mean to press you / on that.

JO: It's fine, Lara.

LARA: And look out for the asphalt.

JO stops, almost out of the room.

LARA: Like, y'know, don't trip / on it –

JO: I'll see you in a sec.

JO exits, leaving the door open. LARA watches her go, makes sure she has left the corridor, then tentatively gets up and goes to JO's office. She stands in the doorway, settling on the filing cabinets. She starts towards them, opens the tops drawer and begins flicking through; TOM enters, wearing his staff lanyard, holding a tiny tupperware filled with water. Infatuated, non-threatening, he sees her in the doorway.

TOM: Hi.

LARA: Tom, hi.

TOM: Oh. You got glasses.

LARA: What are you doing here?

TOM: I'm tutoring Year Six.

LARA: Not 'til 3.30, though.

TOM: I know.

LARA: That's seven hours away.

TOM: My other sessions got cancelled.

LARA: Ok.

TOM: Most of my kids are on holiday now. So the parents want to give them some time off after exams. Which I think is a great idea, and I still get paid.

LARA: Even though you're not teaching?

TOM: Yeah, it's TruThought's cancellation policy. Not mine. It's fine, they can afford it.

LARA: Sure.

Beat.

LARA: Tom.

TOM: Yeah?

LARA: Why are you here?

TOM: You said today was going to be a big day.

LARA: It is.

TOM: So I thought I could be an extra pair of hands.

LARA: I think we're ok for now.

TOM: And I wanted to give you this.

TOM extends the tiny tupperware.

LARA: What is this?

TOM: Your contact lenses. You left them. Last night. They're in there.

LARA takes the tupperware.

LARA: Are they?

TOM: Yeah, look. There and there. I don't know which is which. Minus one point five, minus one point seven five. I remembered. *(Beat.)* One's a bit bluer than the other. Don't know if that helps.

LARA: You took them off the sink?

TOM: Yeah, I thought you might need them. But now I know you have glasses. *(Beat.)* Still, at least you've got the option.

LARA: Tom, these are daily disposables.

TOM: Right.

LARA: So I throw them away every day. You can't re-wear them.

TOM: I didn't know that.

LARA: Thank you, though. Just, for reference, monthly contacts are much smaller.

TOM: For reference, sure.

LARA: And they need to be in saline solution.

TOM: So this wouldn't have worked anyway.

LARA: Well it depends. Is this saline solution?

TOM: No.

LARA: Then it wouldn't have worked.

TOM: It's just water. *(Beat.)* I know for next time.

LARA: Yeah.

TOM: Next time being, you know, whenever works for you.

LARA: I'm quite busy at the moment.

TOM: Not now, obviously.

LARA: I just mean, it's all about to start and I need / to –

TOM: Sure, yeah, course. I've got stuff to get on with.

TOM sets his backpack on the sofa, begins to take out a notebook and water flask.

LARA: Here?

TOM: Yeah. Is that not ok?

LARA: Just – Jo's coming back in a minute.

TOM: I don't mind.

LARA: I guess I – I just mean what... What are you doing?

TOM: Lesson plan.

LARA: For today?

TOM: Yeah.

LARA: Haven't you done it already?

TOM: Oh, I've done it. I'm just going over it. Honing it.

LARA: Right.

TOM: There's not much to do, really, so if you need a hand with anything / I can...

LARA: It's all under control.

TOM: Before the SATs we were just doing the syllabus, it's a bit more free-form now.

LARA: I just need to check the voicemails and go over this contract –

TOM: You don't mind, do you?

LARA: I don't mind, I'm just busy.

TOM: I don't – ok.

Quiet as LARA picks up the phone and listens to voicemails. TOM reads through his lesson plan. He tries not to look at LARA, but finally gives in.

TOM: How are you doing? Oh, sorry, you're on the phone, sorry.

He waits. LARA notes down absentees whose parents have left voicemails for her, puts the phone down.

TOM: How are you feeling?

LARA: Fine.

TOM: Just, 'cause. I was really feeling those shots earlier.

LARA: Me too.

TOM: *(Reaching into his bag.)* Do you want some Ibuprofen?

LARA: I've had some.

TOM: Smart.

LARA: Thanks, though.

TOM: Shouldn't drink on a school night. Learnt that in Year Eight. *(Beat.)* I didn't drink in Year Eight.

LARA: I know.

Pause. TOM takes some Ibuprofen, drinks from his flask. LARA works through the contract.

TOM: What's the contract?

LARA: Just an agreement with the coach company.

TOM: What for?

LARA: Year Six are going to the Natural History Museum.

TOM: Today?

LARA: M-hm.

TOM: Oh, perfect! We can do a session on dinosaurs.

TOM avidly notes in his notebook.

LARA: Do you know enough about dinosaurs to do that?

TOM: Yeah! And I can do some research, see how much they've absorbed from the trip.

LARA: I thought you had a lesson plan.

TOM: Just to kick things off. It was something my macro tutor used to do at Oxford. We'd start with –

LARA: Sorry – macro?

TOM: Macroeconomics. So, like, we'd start with a discursive treatment of something completely off-topic, tear it to shreds, and then have the tutorial. Just to get everyone in this brutal analytic headspace. We did one about pencils once. *(Beat.)* So we can start with dinosaurs and then do maths.

LARA: So they can get into a brutal analytic headspace?

TOM: Yeah. Do you not think it'll work?

LARA: I just need to make sure they get there first.

TOM: Sure, I'll leave you to it.

Silence. LARA goes back to reading through the contract. TOM plans, gets out his laptop. The school phone rings, LARA picks it up.

LARA: St Barnabas'… Morning, Fiona… Well, thanks…

TOM stands up and begins to look around the room; it's not clear what he's searching for. He's quite distracting.

LARA: Ah, that's a shame. No, of course, I'll just note that down for the register…

Meeting LARA's puzzled looks, TOM makes a typing gesture.

LARA: …I hope he feels better soon. Alright… You too, bye.

She puts the phone down, looks at TOM.

LARA: What are you doing?

TOM: Do you have an ethernet cable?

LARA: We're using all of them.

TOM: I'm just – having trouble with the wifi. It's fine, I'll go to a café later.

Silence again. LARA notes down the absentee and returns to the contract. TOM sips water from his flask.

TOM: Where's Jo?

LARA: She's on playground duty.

TOM nods, then builds himself up to say:

TOM: I had a really nice time last night.

LARA: Oh, Tom…

TOM: What?

LARA: Is that why you're here?

TOM: No, no. I wanted to get my lesson plan ready and run it by Jo. And help out, if I can.

LARA: But you haven't done that before.

TOM: Yeah, but… I did have a nice time last night.

LARA: Me too.

TOM: Yeah?

LARA: Yeah, it was fun, but… You're very young.

TOM: I'm twenty-one.

LARA: Exactly.

TOM: Well, how old are you?

LARA: Twenty-six.

TOM: *(After a moment's hesitation.)* Well, that's barely any difference.

LARA: It's a big difference.

TOM: Look, is this because I still live with my parents?

LARA: No!

TOM: Because I was happy to go back to yours.

LARA: We couldn't go back to / mine, Tom.

TOM: And I'm sorry about my dad.

LARA: It's really fine.

TOM: He's a real morning person.

LARA: This isn't about your parents. I still live with mine.

TOM: See?

LARA: It's a bit different, Tom.

TOM: But I think we need to embrace the idea that our generation will be living with our parents 'til they die, and once we've done that you'll be much more open to the idea of seeing me again.

LARA: *(Breaking it to him.)* Look, Tom. You're sweet.

TOM: Thanks, so are you.

LARA: But things are a bit tricky for me to be, like, dating. Right now.

TOM: Oh, ok. Sure. I understand. *(Beat.)* Have you just come out of something?

LARA: It's stuff at home. Mainly.

TOM: Oh, god, I'm sorry.

LARA: It's nothing [drastic]. We can leave it.

TOM: Leave it at that.

> *Beat. To this point TOM has been semi-jocular. This has thrown him, and he resumes in a slightly more serious fashion.*

TOM: We wouldn't have to date.

LARA: Oh my god.

TOM: Like, we could keep things casual if you wanted that. You know, if you think I'm cute, I think you're that too, and, yeah, but I don't want to – sorry, I'm – we could just do what we did last night. More.

LARA: That still seems quite formal.

TOM: It wouldn't be – how is it formal?

LARA: You just described it in full detail.

> *The phone rings. LARA reaches for it.*

TOM: It can still be informal, though –

> *She picks up the phone, cutting him off.*

LARA: St Barnabas'… Hi, Elise… I'll put you through to him now… One sec… Tony, Elise for you… And did you get my email about the meeting at two? And the fluoro? Brilliant, you're a star.

> *She puts the phone down. The sound of a bell ringing from outside; voices fill the corridors as pupils enter their form classes.*

TOM: Look, if you think I'm immature –

LARA: *(Taking her glasses off and stretching them.)* I don't think you're / immature –

TOM: I'm not –

LARA: We're not discussing this anymore.

TOM: Why?

LARA: Because it's unprofessional.

TOM: I'm here to help. As a colleague.

LARA: A colleague.

TOM: *(Off the glasses.)* You're gonna snap those.

LARA: Tom. Listen. I don't want Jo to know.

TOM: It's fine.

LARA: I don't want anyone to know.

Beat.

TOM: Me neither. And she won't.

LARA: Ok. *(Beat.)* I need to get this done before the driver arrives, I don't even know if we can pay him yet.

TOM: Just let me know if I can make myself useful.

LARA: It might be more useful if you / just [left].

JO enters, bloods kit and two permission slips in hand. She sees TOM.

JO: Hi Tom.

TOM: Hi, Jo.

JO: You're a bit early.

TOM: I wanted to show you my lesson plan.

JO: *(Glancing at the clock.)* It's about a day until you start though.

TOM: My TruThought clients cancelled today, so I thought I'd come in.

JO: Are you going to stay?

TOM: Here?

JO: We don't have a lot of room.

TOM: I'll stay out of the way, you won't even know I'm here.

JO: It's about to get busy.

TOM: I know, if there's anything I can help with…

JO: You can get into the staffroom with your pass.

TOM: Great.

TOM sits on one of the tiny chairs, trying to stay out of the way. JO sets two cheques and permission slips on LARA's desk.

JO: Two cheques, two slips.

LARA: *(Taking them.)* Fantastic.

TOM: School trips are probably the only thing keeping chequebooks alive. *(Beat.)* Just 'cause, you know, they're phasing them out...

JO and LARA look at him briefly.

LARA: Did you ever get a permission slip for Hannah?

JO: Hannah Martin?

LARA: Yeah. I've got a cheque but no slip.

JO: I can't remember off the top of my head.

LARA: *(Reaching for a plastic file.)* It's probably in here, let me just...

JO: Her dad didn't call did he?

LARA: Hannah's? No, not today.

JO: Right.

LARA: Was she not in the playground?

JO: No.

TOM: Is this Year Six Hannah?

LARA: Yeah.

JO: *(To LARA.)* Would you give him a ring –

TOM: *(Simultaneously.)* She's always late.

Beat.

LARA: *(Ignoring TOM.)* Sorry, Jo?

JO: It's fine.

LARA: No, go on.

JO: Really. I'll sort it.

LARA: Ok.

JO turns to go into her office. LARA sets the folder to one side.

LARA: Oh, and just on this contract –

TOM: *(Simultaneously.)* Jo, I was thinking if –

JO: I need to make a really quick phone call.

TOM: Sure, yeah.

JO goes into her office, closes the door. TOM sits down and goes through his lesson plan, LARA files the cheques and finishes reading through the contract. JO picks up the office phone, pulls up a contact list on her computer screen. She begins to put the number into the phone, puts it down. Looks at the bloods kit. She picks up the phone again and dials.

JO: Hello, Mr Martin, it's Jo Fell... Fine, thank you, fine. I was just wondering if Hannah was coming in today... Right... I wouldn't normally, it's only because Year Six have their trip... The Natural History Museum? We sent a letter out at the start of term, it's kind of a reward after SATs... Yes, your wife must have paid it... Sorry, Hannah's mother must have... Well, have you checked her bloods this morning?

She looks at the kit bag.

JO: Her mum left an insulin kit here yesterday morning, it was my understanding you were going to pick that up... There is no tone Mr Martin... Because the whole year is going, and she's missed quite a lot of school already... I'm happy to speak to her, but I don't need to... So long as it's in the next five minutes... Ok, thanks Mr Martin.

JO puts the phone down. Then, under her breath:

JO: Fuck.

She opens the door.

LARA: All ok?

JO: Yeah, just – getting a new dishwasher.

LARA: Oh.

TOM: Nightmare.

JO: Yep. *(To LARA.)* The contract?

LARA: For the coach, yeah, I just wanted to double-check it with you.

JO: Sure.

LARA goes to JO's office, they lower their voices. School business.

JO: Ok. *(Scanning the document.)* We're doing a one-off day fee?

LARA: Yeah, because of traffic.

JO: Wouldn't it be cheaper by the hour?

LARA: They charge for hours stationary.

LARA points JO to the contract conditions.

JO: Not worth the risk.

LARA: That's just how I costed it. We – can't really afford for them to get stuck in traffic.

JO: Sure. Just wanted to check.

LARA: And I factored in slack for two absentees. So the numbers still work if Hannah's not coming.

JO: Hannah's going on the trip.

JO sets the contract on her desk, reaches for a pen. LARA walks to the dividing door.

LARA: *(To JO.)* Just going to get these photocopied.

TOM: I'll do it!

LARA: It's genuinely fine.

TOM: You're busy, I'll do it.

LARA: Ok.

LARA hands TOM the code of conduct.

TOM: How many am I getting?

LARA: Thirty-five.

TOM: Great – oh, Jo, I was thinking, because they're going to the Natural History Museum, I could start the lesson with a bit on dinosaurs?

JO: How much is a bit?

TOM: Just a discussion of what they picked up. I'm gonna put it in the plan and run it by you, if that's ok.

JO: Great, yeah.

TOM: Maybe some stuff they might not have learnt. They now think most dinosaurs had feathers. Velociraptors had feathers.

JO: Lara mentioned that earlier.

TOM: *(Remembering with fondness.)* Oh, yeah, we, uh – yeah.

Beat. TOM turns to look at LARA, who doesn't meet his gaze.

TOM: I'll just go and get this photocopied.

TOM exits. A pause. JO walks into LARA's office with the contract.

JO: Contract looks fine.

LARA: Great, great.

JO: Thanks for that.

LARA: You are welcome. Assembly in five minutes.

JO: Who's taking it today?

LARA: You are.

JO: Yes I am.

LARA's office phone rings. JO walks to her office.

JO: Patch that through to me, I know who it is.

LARA: Dishwasher guy?

JO: Yeah.

JO closes her office door as LARA patches the call. JO's phone rings once and she picks it up. Her eyes hover on the bloods kit.

JO: Hello Mr Martin? Yes, do put her on… Hello Hannah, it's Ms Fell… Now, Hannah, are you feeling poorly? Have you checked your blood sugars… Yes I've got the kit here, you can come and pick it up when dad drops you off… And you know you're going to the Natural History Museum today? Don't be sorry! You don't have to say sorry… Ok, well put dad back on… Alright… Bye bye Hannah… Hello… Yes… It sounds like we need to check her bloods, but if you don't have a kit… Yes, we can check them here…

A bell rings for assembly.

JO: We may need to discuss with the three of you how we're managing her diabetes at home… How you're managing, the pair of you… I can't now, I have assembly. No, that's not – I have to make sure my pupils are safe, Mr Martin… Well there's a permission slip you'll need to sign when you get here… For the trip, yes… I'll have one waiting –

JO's phone call ends. TOM enters LARA'S office with the photocopied sheets and several registers.

TOM: Here are the codes of conduct.

LARA: Thanks.

TOM: And the registers. Picked them up from the staffroom.

LARA: Oh. Cheers.

TOM: No problem. And sorry if I / said something [wrong].

JO enters LARA's office.

JO: Right, assembly Lara?

LARA: Coming now. And I found a time, Friday at 10 for the governors' meeting?

JO: Perfect.

LARA: *(Writing another post-it.)* I'll send an email out. What are you going to do?

JO: The good samaritan, I think.

LARA: Nice.

TOM: Good call.

Beat.

JO: Any birthdays?

LARA: *(Getting a box of celebrations from the filing cabinet.)* Yeah, Hisham in Year 2 and Georgie Hughes in Year 4.

JO: Have we got enough in there?

LARA: *(Shaking the box.)* Yep.

TOM: Sorry, you know who they are?

JO: Hisham and Georgie? Yes.

TOM: Wow.

JO: Why?

TOM: No, nothing, it's just – my headmaster didn't know me by name. Or sight.

JO: We try our best. Do you want to come to assembly?

TOM: Oh, I won't, thanks. I'm not a big 'god' guy.

JO: Sure. It's not too 'god'.

TOM: I mean, I'm sure it'll be great.

JO: Thanks.

TOM: I'll get on with some stuff here. And if you need anything doing, either of you –

JO: I think we're sorted for now, thanks.

LARA: Me too.

TOM: Sure. Any tea, coffee?

JO: I'm good. See you in fifteen minutes.

TOM: Cool.

JO and LARA exit, and TOM sits on the sofa. At the door, LARA turns.

LARA: Tom?

TOM: Yeah?

LARA: I could go for a cup of tea.

TOM: On it.

LARA: Thanks.

TOM: You're welcome, sugar? *(Aware this sounds like 'You're welcome, sugar.')* Do you take sugar?

LARA: *(Smiling.)* Just milk, please.

TOM nods, LARA exits. He smiles and flicks the kettle on. As he stands to make the teas, LARA's phone rings. He turns to the door, but LARA and JO are long gone. He stares at the phone, unable to answer. As he waits for the ringing to stop:

End of Act 1.

Interstitial

The kettle boils. TOM pours a cup of tea.

TONY, dressed in work overalls and a baseball cap, passes the doorway in the corridor carrying a stepladder. He enters, empties the bins into a large bin liner, looks at the flickering light for a moment, then exits.

The clocks on the office walls are changed to 12.15pm. TOM exits. JO and LARA rip open the letters in their post grilles. LARA exits.

Act 2

12.15pm. Lunch break. The murmur of the playground.

JO sits at her desk, her office door shut. The bloods kit is still on her desk. Also on the desk are a flask of soup, an apple and a bottle of water. JO is finishing the soup while reading the files from the Local Authority meeting.

She glances at the phone. Then reaches for it and plays the voicemail. As it plays, LARA enters from the corridor, carrying a tray with a plate of chicken and salad, with sachets of salad dressing on the tray.

VOICEMAIL: Hello, only me. I can't get through on the mobile so I thought I'd try you here, you must, um – not be in yet. I know it's not ideal, but you're not picking up at home either, so... Yep.

LARA sets the tray on her desk, checks her email. She goes towards JO's office door.

VOICEMAIL: Just checking you were all set for tomorrow, might be nice to talk to you without the solicitor. I found the marriage certificate, so you can stop looking for that. If you were looking. I'll try again later. And they said it wouldn't / take long –

LARA: Jo?

JO immediately lifts up the receiver, silencing the voicemail. As she does so:

JO: Can I have a minute?

LARA: Sorry, didn't know you were in here –

JO: That's ok.

LARA: Sorry.

LARA goes back to her desk and begins to read from a textbook. Silence.

JO: Damn.

The phone on JO's desk rings. She reaches towards it – then sends the call to voicemail. She rounds her desk and goes to LARA's office.

JO: Lara, if you get a call / from –

LARA: I'm so sorry about that –

JO: It's ok, just –

LARA: I should have knocked –

JO: Well, next time.

LARA: Yeah. I didn't mean to disturb.

JO: That's – it's fine.

LARA: Ok.

JO: No harm done.

> *Beat.*

LARA: If I get a call from…?

> *JO considers briefly.*

JO: Yeah. You know what, forward all calls to me.

LARA: What?

JO: Forward calls to me. For the next hour or so.

> *Beat.*

JO: It's your lunch break. I've finished. It's cool.

> *LARA presses several buttons on her phone.*

JO: Don't want you being hassled by the washing machine people.

LARA: I thought it was your dishwasher?

> *LARA's mobile begins to ring loudly. She checks it and puts it down, turns it onto vibrate.*

JO: You can take that.

LARA: No, it's fine.

JO: You're on your lunch break.

LARA: I know.

> *The mobile continues to vibrate. LARA turns it off, plays with her glasses. The vibration stops.*

LARA: I just – I want to finish this chapter.

JO: *(Off the book.)* Don't stress about that. It's not worth it.

LARA: I'm not.

JO: You are. You're doing that thing with your glasses.

LARA: *(Putting down her glasses.)* No I'm not.

JO: Old habits.

LARA: I didn't think you'd remember that.

JO: You never forget your first class. Terrifying.

LARA: It wasn't that long ago.

JO: No, it's not that, it's just you were awful. Not you, exactly. *(She considers.)* Though you had your moments.

LARA: I was eleven.

JO: Well, exactly.

> *LARA's phone vibrates again. She picks it up, turns it off and puts it into a desk drawer.*

LARA: So that was when you realized this stuff wasn't worth it?

JO: Not pointless, it's just not for real kids.

LARA: Right. So how about... *(Reading.)* 'in the case of sustained disruption from one child, establish a three warning system before separating them in the classroom.'

JO: Well, two problems there.

LARA: Only two?

JO: You haven't got room to separate one child from the others, firstly. You won't be training in a classroom with fewer than twenty five pupils.

LARA: Yeah, I kind of suspected that.

JO: And you can't send them out, because that's just a waste of time, and they're even more distracting when they're pulling faces through the door, or wandering around the corridor singing.

LARA: Singing?

JO: Yeah, pop songs, just making everyone laugh. In fairness it is very funny. But that's the other problem, separating them gives them the attention they wanted in the first place.

LARA: So the three warning system?

JO: Can work…

LARA: *(Holding up textbook.)* I'll just burn this.

JO: If you really need silence, use the stare.

LARA: The stare?

> *LARA looks at JO, who briefly turns her head away, snaps her head back towards LARA with narrowed eyes and an impassive expression. LARA remembers in a flood of nostalgia and terror.*

LARA: The stare!

JO: Yeah.

LARA: I buried that.

JO: *(Breaking the stare.)* Sorry.

LARA: Shit.

JO: *(Pleased.)* I know, right?

LARA: When did you work that out?

JO: With you lot. I had all those techniques, and they worked at St Michael's, when I had a mentor in the room. But then when you're on your own –

LARA: I think I'll use it.

JO: It's all yours. Takes practice though. Years.

LARA: Can I try?

JO: Sure.

LARA: *(Standing up, demonstrating behind her desk.)* Ok, so I'm writing on the board, you're talking, I'm asking a question –

JO: I'm still talking.

LARA: Ask you nicely to stop.

JO: Still talking though.

LARA: Give you a warning.

JO: Don't care, still talking.

LARA: And stare.

LARA stares at JO. It's not convincing.

JO: It's good Lara.

LARA: Yeah?

JO: Scary. But wider stance. And you can narrow your eyebrows more.

LARA: *(Taking a note.)* I don't know if I can do that.

JO: Comes with age.

Beat.

JO: You're not still trawling through Ofsted reports, are you?

LARA: Finished those.

JO: Thank god.

LARA: Just the textbooks now.

JO: I'd just get on with it and apply.

LARA: I know, I just – I want to be ready this time.

JO: You're still going this year?

LARA: Depends on stuff with dad. But yeah, hopefully.

JO: I think you should.

LARA: I think I will. *(Beat.)* Where did you train?

JO: St Michael's. Straight out of uni.

LARA: I thought you were an accountant for a bit.

JO: Oh, that doesn't really count.

LARA: Why not?

JO: Because I didn't care.

LARA: It was still your job, though.

JO: Jumped before I was pushed.

Half-beat.

LARA: Where's St Michael's?

JO: Wandsworth, next to Battersea Park.

LARA: How is it? As a place to train?

JO: Not as good as here.

Beat.

LARA: 'Cause I've got that thing – I just want to be in front of a class again. It's pretty pointless to be learning pupil management techniques when I'm not teaching any of them.

JO: It's good to do the reading. But they're not like they are in the books.

LARA's office phone rings.

JO: I thought you were forwarding calls to me –

LARA: I know, they should be.

JO: I'll get that –

Before she can get to the phone LARA answers.

LARA: St Barnabas'… Oh, hi there… She is, just hold on one second.

LARA transfers the call, a light on JO's phone starts to flash.

JO: Who is it?

LARA: Local Authority.

JO: James?

LARA nods. JO closes her office door.

JO: Shit.

JO picks up the phone.

JO: Hi James, it's Jo… No problem… Sure… Just give me one second.

JO goes to her office door, pulls it shut. LARA keeps her eyes on her books.

JO: You could have told me there'd be a broker in the meeting, Jim… He had no reason to be there… We're an improving school – yes, according to Ofsted. They need to prove that we're not meeting progress standards to even suggest it, and that's not on the table at the moment… No. I will not be talking to his list of sponsors. Because we don't meet the criteria. I am a bit… Because you know we can't support a wider catchment area, and you know that gives them grounds to turn us into an academy... It's a funding cut in everything but the word – he was in the bloody room, James! His eyes lit up, he smelt blood, he literally licked his lips... I don't care if it's a condition. *(Beat.)* I know it's not your fault, but I thought you were on my side. Tell me what I can do, then. *(Her eyes dart to the filing cabinet. Beat.)* I haven't seen the results yet... I'll let you know as soon as I do... I'll check.

She puts the phone to her shoulder, stares straight ahead. Two deep breaths, three. She doesn't look at the computer. She puts the phone back to her ear.

JO: I'm having problems logging in... The server's probably... Overloaded. Maybe it's my login. I'll try again in a bit. No, no I'll check with my office. Ok... How good would they have to be? To be safe? *(Beat.)* Ok. Yeah, I understand. We'll know by tomorrow, then... I will... Enjoy your lunch-break.

JO slams the phone down, letting the receiver slip off the base and onto the desk.

JO: Can we make sure calls come through directly to me?

LARA: Yep, sorry, I think I pressed the wrong button.

JO: So they're coming through to me now?

LARA: Yeah, yeah.

JO: Just – while you're on your break.

Beat.

JO: You should train here.

LARA: Oh. Really?

JO: It's close to home, the kids know you. You can be on call for your dad.

LARA: Thanks, Jo. But I haven't even applied yet. Reapplied.

JO: You're going back to Southside?

LARA: Same college, yeah.

43

JO: We've had training placements through them before. I can give them a call.

LARA: You don't have to.

JO: But you should apply soon if you want to start this year.

LARA: I know.

JO: You're ready. If you want me to have a look at your application –

LARA: It's just I think it's done internally – the placements.

JO: But I can put in a word.

LARA: I'll definitely think about it.

JO: Just, whatever makes your life easier.

LARA: Cheers. This has already made it loads easier.

JO: We needed another person on the team. Your dad and I didn't really have time for a proper handover.

LARA: That couldn't be helped.

JO: No. I sometimes have to remind myself this isn't temporary.

LARA: He wasn't involved... In getting me this, was he?

JO: Your dad?

LARA: Yeah.

JO: No. You applied, you got it.

LARA: Ok.

JO: I wouldn't have bothered with the interviews otherwise.

LARA: I know. I knew that.

JO: Good. No rush on the placement. Just let me know.

LARA: I will, Jo.

JO: And – last thing – you wouldn't have to carry on with this while you're training. You could, if you wanted to.

LARA: Might be a struggle.

JO: But this isn't what you want to do.

LARA: What do you mean?

JO: This. Is it, really?

LARA: I love it here, Jo.

JO: But you want to teach.

LARA: Yeah, eventually.

JO: So take the job.

LARA: The job?

JO: The offer.

LARA: I haven't even got in.

JO: You will do.

LARA: But what if I don't?

JO: You will do.

LARA: What if you get someone better?

JO: Lara.

LARA: I mean it, there'll be loads of applicants.

JO: Why wouldn't you take it?

LARA: Because it wouldn't be fair.

JO: You'd fit in really well, you know I'm flexible.

LARA: But I went here. I work here. And it's my dad's.

    Beat.

LARA: He's still a governor –

JO: Your dad's what?

LARA: School.

JO: Right.

LARA: For me, I mean.

JO: Right.

LARA: I just think I need to see others. Be somewhere else.

JO: This is a good school, Lara.

LARA: I know, that's not it –

JO: Students want to train here. And I know your dad's always been keen for you / to –

LARA: I know.

JO: You know?

LARA: Yeah.

JO: Oh.

LARA: I don't think I should train here.

JO: Have you told him?

LARA: Couple of days ago.

JO: How did that...?

LARA: It came up over tea.

JO: No, I mean how did he take it?

LARA: Oh. *(Beat.)* You know him.

JO: Right.

LARA: Yeah.

JO: I just want good teachers. *(Half-beat.)* I want teachers.

LARA: If you've got time I'd – I'd love some help on the application.

JO: Yeah, of course.

JO gently turns the bloods kit on her desk.

LARA: Did Hannah make the trip?

JO: Just. Her dad took her to the chemist's, picked up another one of these. *(Holds up the kit)* Thank god. We had to hold the bus at the gates. He wouldn't even get out of his bloody car. Can you believe that?

LARA: At least she made it.

JO: It shouldn't be like that. It's manageable.

LARA: Her mum seems pretty clued up.

JO: Her mum's not the problem.

LARA: When did you speak to him?

JO: Just at the gates, this morning. Tony was right about the asphalt, by the way.

LARA: Oh. You said he didn't get out of the car.

JO: He didn't.

LARA: So when did you speak to him?

JO: On the phone, before.

LARA: He called to mark her down as absent?

JO: No, he'd never bother.

LARA: So... You called him?

JO: Yeah. Why?

LARA: Nothing, it's just I do that. Usually.

JO: But this is a repeat problem.

LARA: Yeah, I know, just – I usually make the absence calls after assembly.

JO: I know.

LARA: When I've done the registers.

JO: It's a bit of a delicate situation, with them.

LARA: I've called Hannah's parents before, I could have rung them today.

JO: You could, but... I'm concerned. About her.

LARA: Ok. How concerned?

Beat.

LARA: I mean, do we register it as a Safeguarding Issue?

JO: That's too far.

Beat.

LARA: I can understand him trying not to make a big deal of it.

JO: He's doing nothing. She's the only diabetic pupil in the school, and / she's not –

LARA: And you've given all the staff training. She's safe here.

JO: Here, yeah. I'm not being over-protective.

47

LARA: No. It's in the bloody Children's Act.

JO: Right.

LARA: But you can't monitor every parent. It's their kids you've got to worry about.

JO: *(Off the books.)* Revision is going well.

LARA: Do you think you might be doing too much?

JO: No such thing.

LARA: You can delegate to me.

JO: I'm fine, Lara.

LARA: You didn't tell him to bring Hannah in, did you?

JO: What? No, no.

LARA: Because that's – I mean, we can't do that.

JO: I know.

LARA: I can talk to social services, it'd just be a visit –

JO: We're not there yet, Lara.

LARA: Ok, well if we're not, then – you can let me do my job. I can do it. And with Hannah, you've done all you can.

JO: Ok.

LARA: Burnout is a thing.

JO: I'm not sure they call it that anymore.

LARA: Well, I've seen it.

JO: So have I, but I'm not him.

Beat.

LARA: No.

JO: Sorry.

LARA: Don't be, do you need me to get moving on the results? I'm thinking the sooner we submit for the award the better.

JO: Not for now, no.

LARA: Really? I've got the Department for Education site up, I can start the application now.

JO: We'll wait until after the governors' meeting.

LARA: Ok. But I will need to know the results.

JO: Why?

LARA: So I can tell them the agenda in the email.

JO: I won't be discussing them with anyone until after the meeting. Sorry, Lara.

LARA: That means we won't be able to get onto it 'til Monday. Don't we need to start processing it as soon as possible?

A light on LARA's phone starts to flash. She looks across to JO's phone, whose light is also flashing. JO follows LARA's line of sight.

LARA: That might be Sarah.

JO: It's the dishwasher people. Sarah called earlier.

LARA: It might still be her, though.

JO: No, the booking went through fine. Back at 3.30. They'll be a bit late for Tom's session.

LARA: Oh. I'll let him know.

A beat as they watch the red light stop flashing.

LARA: Your phone's off the hook.

JO: Oh, yeah. Thanks.

JO goes to her desk, hastily replaces the receiver. It slips off again; she goes to put it back but can't bring herself to do it.

JO: Why's he here, by the way?

LARA: Who?

JO: Tom.

LARA: I don't know. He's not here. I don't know where he is.

JO: I know, but why is he here?

LARA: He said he's planning – he's 'refining' his lesson plan.

JO: That the only reason?

Beat.

LARA: I told him to leave.

JO: I don't care.

LARA: I think he's just keen to help.

JO: He'd better not invoice us for the whole day.

LARA: I don't think he'd do that.

JO: Well, you know him better than I do.

LARA: I really don't.

JO: So long as it's not affecting work, I really don't mind.

LARA: It's not even [a thing] – it hasn't. It won't.

JO: Good.

LARA: I didn't want him here.

TOM enters carrying two Carluccio's bags. JO goes into her office.

TOM: Hello.

LARA: Hi Tom.

A bell rings in the playground. The voices fall briefly, then rise again as pupils return inside.

TOM: Hi. *(Going to JO's office as LARA slides her phone into her desk drawer.)* Hi Jo.

JO: Hello.

TOM: How's it going?

JO: Fine thanks, just going over some things.

TOM: *(Catching the L.A. on the board.)* Meeting in Hollywood?

JO: Oh, that's Local Authority. The council.

TOM: Yep, the council, I know, it was a… Doesn't matter. How was it? Good news?

JO: *(Hesitates.)* Just news.

TOM: Cool.

JO: Yeah.

TOM: Whenever you're done I've got the lesson plan to run by you. Should be a fun one, I think.

JO: Great, I'll give you a shout in a bit.

TOM: Awesome.

TOM pushes JO's office door to. Then, to LARA, quietly:

TOM: Hey, I called you.

LARA: Oh, I turned my mobile off. Sorry.

TOM: *(Getting a pot of salad out of one of the bags.)* Yeah, I didn't know what you wanted for lunch, so I got you a chicken caesar salad. Bit boring.

LARA: Oh, Tom. I've already eaten. Sorry.

Her plate is mostly untouched. TOM registers this.

TOM: Oh, no, that's fine. Jo, do you want a chicken caesar salad?

JO: Got soup, thanks Tom.

TOM: From Carluccio's. There you go. Double lunch for me. Got a cake as well, don't know if you wanted it.

LARA: Maybe in a bit.

TOM: Cool, cool.

TOM goes and sits on the sofa and begins to unpack his salad. In her office, JO reviews the Local Authority files and types up headteacher's letters for the reports. She can hear everything TOM and LARA say.

TOM: I haven't had lunch at school in ages. *(Beat.)* Did you make that?

LARA: It's from the caf.

TOM: The one outside?

LARA: The school cafeteria.

TOM: What did you get?

LARA: Chicken and salad.

TOM: Ah, so I was on the right track. Is it good?

LARA: Chicken and leaves, you know.

TOM: Sure, yeah.

Beat. TOM eats. The fluoro flickers.

TOM: I think the fluorescent's broken.

LARA: Yeah, it is.

TOM: I can take a look at it.

LARA: Tony's going to fix it later today.

TOM: Tony?

LARA: The caretaker.

TOM: Oh, right. Cool. *(Beat.)* Probably a bad transformer.

> *Neither of them knows what that means. LARA holds out the olive branch.*

LARA: What did you get?

TOM: *(With his mouth full.)* This is a goat's cheese and beetroot salad.

LARA: Is it good?

TOM: It's great! Do you want to try some?

LARA: I'm fine, thanks. Full.

> *Beat.*

TOM: Working lunch?

LARA: Yeah.

TOM: Anything I can do?

LARA: Not really, I'm studying.

TOM: What for?

LARA: PGCE.

TOM: Teacher training?

LARA: Yeah.

TOM: That's amazing!

> *JO snorts.*

LARA: Thanks.

TOM: While you're doing this?

LARA: I'm applying, it's early stages.

TOM: So this isn't part of the course?

LARA: No this is just… My job.

TOM: Wow. How long's the course?

LARA: Just a year.

TOM: Does Jo know?

JO looks up, towards LARA's office. The ring of a bell; voices steadily fill the playground again.

LARA: Yeah, she's been really supportive.

TOM: Oh. Yeah, I bet. And it doesn't affect stuff here?

LARA: I just read whenever I get the chance. Work comes first, you know?

TOM: Yeah, 'course. That's so cool though. *(Beat.)* You didn't tell me.

LARA: I guess it just hasn't come up before.

TOM: Right. I dunno, just, it's something I would be proud of. You're proud of it, right?

LARA: Not really. It's just what I want to do.

TOM: Cool. *(Beat.)* Must be good to know.

LARA: Are you not going to go into tutoring?

TOM: No. This is a – I don't want to say stopgap.

LARA: But it's a stopgap.

TOM: Yeah. I mean this isn't a career. It doesn't go… Anywhere.

Beat. JO has stopped typing, listening in.

LARA: Would you consider teaching?

TOM: I start law school in September.

LARA: I see.

TOM: More higher education.

LARA: Yeah.

TOM: Maybe teaching in a few years. I'll keep tutoring on the side.

LARA: Pay the fees, right?

TOM: No, I've got a contract with a firm, they cover the course. But the living grant's a little thin, so I'll tutor as well. Keep me in ubers and Haribo.

LARA: It's still a kind of teaching though, isn't it?

TOM: Maybe. I haven't really thought about it. I mean I'm a tutor. Teachers are people who actually do it. Full time.

Beat. JO returns to typing.

LARA: You didn't mention law last night.

TOM: I don't know anything about it yet.

LARA: Fair.

TOM: And it's not exactly scintillating conversation.

LARA: But if it's what you want to do…

TOM: Yeah. Yeah.

Beat.

TOM: You'll be really good.

LARA: How do you know?

TOM: Dunno, just a feeling. When will you start, like, properly?

LARA: On the course. Half of it's in classrooms.

TOM: So you learn as you go?

LARA: Kind of, yeah.

TOM: I remember my first lesson. Scary, but fun. 'Cause, you know, they came in…

LARA: That's a good start.

TOM: Yeah.

Beat.

TOM: But they kept coming in. I didn't think thirty-two was a big number. It's like – a huge number. And little things escalate.

JO and LARA both look up.

LARA: Escalate?

TOM: Yeah. Get worse.

LARA: What do you mean?

TOM: Dunkergate.

LARA: Dunkergate?

TOM: Yeah, Dairylea Dunkergate. Basically, um, the twins – Archie and Seb?

LARA: I know them, yeah.

TOM: Had a pack of Dairylea Dunkers each, and they opened them at the same time. Suddenly everyone wants a Dunker.

LARA: What did you do?

TOM: I was drawing up decimals on the board when they opened them. I thought everyone was excited about moving place units across. They weren't. They were excited about the Dunkers. And they were salt and vinegar flavour, so the smell's everywhere... And they're all like 'where's my Dunker?' They think I've given the twins their Dunkers. I haven't. I didn't want anyone to have a Dunker.

LARA: So you confiscated them?

TOM: Yeah, I thought I could combine punishment for having the Dunkers with a kind of reward in a redistributional model –

LARA: Ok.

TOM: So I said everyone could have a Dunker when they finished converting their decimals into fractions. Genius, I thought. Wasn't. They finish the exercise at different times. And then people who've finished ask for Dunkers, and people who haven't finished are upset when they don't get Dunkers, and they can't concentrate on the sums because the person next to them is enjoying their Dunker, and then I'm just a Dunker dispenser and the cheese runs out so people are eating Dunkers without cheese and they're too dry and they're asking if they can go and get water and then the Dunkers ran out. Shitstorm.

LARA: Wow.

TOM: Yeah. That was my first lesson.

Beat. TOM regains composure. JO stands, finishes her bottle of water. Then she goes to the board, puts a tick next to 'Year 2 Headteacher's Reports.' The lights on both phones flash. LARA moves to alert JO, but TOM continues:

TOM: I called my mum afterwards. Just to tell her I had a newfound respect for her profession.

LARA: Your mum's a teacher?

TOM: Yeah.

LARA: Where does she teach?

TOM: Winchester. If you want her email I'm sure she'd be happy to chat.

JO peeks through the dividing door. Both phones flash again.

LARA: Oh, thanks.

TOM: Not that I want you to meet my mum. Not like that, anyway. But, you've already met my dad, / so –

LARA: I got it.

TOM: Just, she'd be able to give you some tips. She's big on technology, interactive stuff. They've all got iPads.

Beat. JO returns to her desk. She sees the light flashing.

TOM: I've got a couple of lessons I'm actually quite proud of.

LARA: Oh yeah?

TOM: I don't know if you can teach this, because a lot of it was improvised, but maybe as, like, a case study. If you're still thinking theoretically.

LARA: I love a bit of theory.

LARA closes her book and sets it aside. TOM notices. JO hesitates before the phone, then returns to the Local Authority files.

TOM: Sorry, unless you need to, revise, / or…

LARA: No, run me through it.

TOM: Um, okay. Great. I'm just thinking… *(He looks around for a surface.)* 'Cause I did this on the whiteboard – *(He spots LARA's board behind her desk.)* Perfect, we can use this.

He wipes the board clean with his sleeve. JO wipes LA meeting off her whiteboard.

LARA: I – ok.

TOM: Ok, ready?

LARA: Sure.

TOM spots a framed photo on her desk.

TOM: Is that...?

LARA: My dad.

TOM: Sure, your dad. He's very young.

LARA: He's older now.

TOM: Right.

LARA: The photo was taken in the past.

TOM: Tautology. *(Beat.)* Sorry. *(Looking at the photo again.)* Hey, that's 6S, isn't it?

LARA: Er, yeah, think so.

TOM: Was he a teacher here?

LARA: Headteacher.

JO returns to the door.

TOM: Amazing. For how long?

LARA: Seventeen years.

TOM: Is he somewhere else now?

LARA: He's a governor. He retired two years ago.

TOM: Ah. So no overlap.

LARA: Not while I've been working here.

TOM: You went here?

LARA: Yeah.

TOM: And he was your headmaster?

LARA: For my last three years, yeah.

TOM: You didn't tell me you went here! Did I just monologue yesterday...?

He trails off as LARA glances towards JO's office, eyes widened at TOM, exasperated. JO draws away from the door. TOM continues more quietly.

TOM: Sorry, it's just because, I was gonna say, that's another thing – we've got that in common. I was at school while my mum was teaching there.

LARA: Right.

Beat.

LARA: It's not great is it?

TOM: It sucks. *(Beat.)* Is he glad you're working here?

LARA: I think so.

TOM: Good headmaster?

LARA: He was great.

JO smiles.

TOM: He looks like you, here. Or, you look like him. *(Beat.)* Sorry. The lesson. Er, you might want to sit over there, so you can see the board.

LARA: Ok.

LARA moves to the chairs opposite the sofa. JO sits at her desk, searches through her bag for ibuprofen. She pops two tablets onto the desk, but finds her water bottle empty.

TOM: That's rule number one, incidentally, crucial that everyone can see what you're doing.

LARA: I'll note that down.

TOM: *(Gesturing to LARA's glasses.)* You can see with those, right?

LARA: Just about.

TOM: Ok, so for context, this was in May.

JO starts at the mention of the month.

TOM: The lesson started with literary devices. So like simile, metaphor, personification, alliteration, rhyme. That took about fifteen minutes / and then –

LARA: Fifteen minutes?

TOM: Yeah.

LARA: You covered that in fifteen minutes? With eleven year olds?

TOM: It was just a recap. I've only got an hour, and they've covered most of it.

LARA: Okay.

JO is listening closely.

TOM: So yeah, literary devices – focus points, that's what they're called on the curriculum. Have you gotten around to that yet?

LARA: The new curriculum?

TOM: Yeah. New?

LARA: Since last year.

TOM: Oh, 'course, yeah. Well, hot tip: BBC Bitesize. Really useful.

JO goes to her computer, a quick search.

LARA: Cool.

TOM: Yeah, so those, and then grammar – adjectives and pronouns. And then, this is where it gets fun, you know 'The Wall'?

LARA: In the classroom?

TOM: No, like Pink Floyd. 'The Wall Part Two'.

LARA: Yeah?

TOM: 'We don't need no education,' that one? I played them that.

LARA: Why?

TOM begins scribbling the lyrics of Pink Floyd's 'The Wall Pt. II' on the whiteboard. JO looks from the computer to the dividing wall.

TOM: Grammar. It all comes back to grammar. And this just came to me on the spur of the moment, I'd been listening to it on the tube, I think.

LARA: So you didn't plan it?

TOM: It just came to me. Sometimes you just see how to make things come to life. Grammar's boring, you know?

He has finished writing up the lyrics to the first verse and chorus. As he speaks he circles, underlines and corrects words as appropriate.

TOM: Ok, so, we start with the disenchanted but somehow enchanting opening drawl – 'we don't need no education.' Now, 'no' here is an adjective meaning 'not any,' modifying its noun 'education.' So we went through what that sentence means grammatically, which is 'we don't need not any education,' i.e., 'we need education' which, we agreed, was probably not Mr Waters' intention.

LARA: Sure.

TOM: But we also agreed that, like all literature, it's open to interpretation. We can't say what Mr Waters should have written, but to avoid the double negative, he should have used 'any' instead of 'no.' Hannah suggested that. So, 'any' can function as an adjective and pronoun governing an amount of the noun, 'education'. Roger doesn't need any education. Though ironically, his sentence composition suggests that he does. Then we discussed irony. Briefly.

LARA: Irony's not on the syllabus, is it?

TOM: No, but… They should know about it, I think. *(Beat.)* Then we get to the next big clanger. 'Hey, teacher!'

JO stands.

LARA: Leave them kids alone.

TOM: Yeah. Now, they spotted the issue here, so I know you can.

LARA: 'Them.'

TOM: The use of the pronoun 'them.' We don't need it! Because we've already got 'kids' in the sentence. If we didn't have the specifying noun, we could say 'leave them alone.' But we do have the specifying noun, here. So we really ought to have the demonstrative 'those' as an adjective modifying the noun we already have.

LARA: Was that all / you did–

60

TOM: And ironically – sorry – the kids singing in the second chorus get it right. They do say 'hey, teacher, leave those kids alone!' So perhaps the kids are less in need of education than Roger. And that was where we left it. Irony again.

JO grips her office chair hard.

LARA: Did they like it?

TOM: I mean Pink Floyd isn't for everyone. And they weren't born. But yeah, I think so. *(Beat.)* And I've got one on storytelling where I showed them the opening of *Gladiator* –

LARA: Sorry, Tom.

TOM: Yeah?

LARA: Just, when did you say this was?

TOM: This lesson?

LARA: Yeah.

TOM: May. Early May, the fourth, I think.

LARA: Oh. *(Beat.)* Their SATs were in May.

JO pauses. Then she takes a small water-can from the top of her filing cabinet and begins to water the potted plants dotted around the room. As she does so:

TOM: Yeah.

LARA: They were meant to be revising.

TOM: This was revision.

LARA: Of what?

TOM: Grammar. *(Gesturing to board.)* Like, nouns, adjectives, pronouns.

LARA: I just don't know if it's appropriate.

TOM: It's Roger Waters' finest work, I don't / think –

LARA: But how is it appropriate if pupils are leaving this school singing 'we don't need no education'?

TOM: It's just a song.

LARA: Did you assess their understanding?

61

TOM: Sorry, I'm not so hot on the jargon, 'assess their understanding'?

LARA: Of the grammar. The nouns, pronouns, adjectives.

TOM: You just mean did I test them?

LARA: Yeah, a formative assessment.

TOM: I didn't test them right then, if that's what you mean.

LARA: So how do you know they learnt anything?

TOM: They were enjoying it.

LARA: Yeah but, how do you know they could read the words on the board?

TOM: I gave them a test the week after. I think.

LARA: But the English SAT was on the tenth of May.

JO finishes watering the plants. She takes a look around the room, then swiftly goes to her office door.

TOM: What do you mean?

LARA: Well, they'd done the SAT by the next time you saw them. So that was the last session before their English test.

TOM: Then I'm remembering wrong, this lesson must have been in April. Late April.

JO pushes open her office door.

JO: Can I see?

TOM: Hi, Jo. Um, see what?

JO: Your lesson plan. I've got a few minutes now.

TOM: Ok.

He retrieves a sheet of paper and his laptop. He presents the sheet to JO.

TOM: Here we are. Algebra.

JO: This is from BBC Bitesize.

TOM: Yeah. That's just a framework. I've got notes in the margins.

JO: The BBC Bitesize pages are archived.

TOM: How d'you mean?

JO: They're not updated anymore.

TOM: Oh.

JO: So they're not up to date with the national curriculum. They didn't change with the new syllabus.

TOM: I haven't been using it for every session.

JO: Can I see your other plans?

TOM: You've never asked for them before.

JO: But they'll be on your laptop. You use that for everything, don't you?

TOM: *(Opening his laptop.)* Well, yeah I've got this plan about dinosaur evolution.

JO: I want to see what you've been teaching them on the syllabus.

TOM: I've been using the Key Stage 2 revision guides for most of it, going through that.

JO: When were the guides published?

TOM: I don't know. Why?

JO: The curriculum changed. This is its second year.

TOM: Yeah. I know.

JO: So were the guides up to date?

TOM: I didn't just use those –

JO: Were they?

TOM: I don't know.

JO: So no plans of your own?

TOM: Yes. My plans – I've been trying to teach them things they wouldn't get in a normal lesson. Going beyond the curriculum.

JO: But those classes, Tom, they were for the SATs. To get them on… An equal footing.

TOM: Who with?

JO: Their 'advantaged peers.' The ones you're busy getting into grammar schools.

TOM: I marched against grammar schools.

JO: Why? It's just another hour to you, isn't it?

The lights on both phones flash.

LARA: Um, Jo —

JO turns, sees her phone lighting up, and starts towards her office.

JO: *(To LARA.)* I've got it.

TOM: SATs just test teachers. It's not something the pupils should have to worry about.

JO: You don't control that.

TOM: They don't mean anything.

JO: Tell that to the parents.

JO reaches the phone as the flashing stops.

TOM: I tell it to the kids.

JO: You what?

TOM: I remind them. Every session. The tests don't matter. Everyone else knows it, why shouldn't they?

JO: Their parents are paying. For those sessions.

TOM: Sorry, no. I'm not sure that's right. I'm paid through the agency.

JO: Who are paid through the pupil premium, which isn't enough when you factor in the agency's commission.

TOM: But the pupil premium is the grant. I understood that's how I'm paid.

JO: It's for kids on free school meals but it's per child —

TOM: Yeah, I know what it is.

JO: — and not every pupil in that class is on free school meals. So the premium itself isn't enough to cover costs. Parents picked up the shortfall. They paid you.

TOM: Ok, TruThought never made that clear in the contract.

JO: Because they don't know. They just take their cut.

TOM: This was my understanding: I'm there to help with literacy and numeracy, but also as a mentor. That was my brief, broaden their / horizons –

JO: This isn't Dead Poets'. You can't swan in and expect to inspire them.

TOM: I didn't expect to inspire them, I was just teaching.

JO: *(Gesturing to the board.)* That? That is pedantry in pop music, it's trivia.

TOM: If you didn't like what I was doing why didn't you just talk / to me?

JO: Because I don't have time to check up on you, Tom. I'm running a school. I've got two hundred pupils and we're going to have a wider catchment area than ever starting next year. That's the good news from the Local Authority.

TOM: I'm just wondering why you / wouldn't –

JO: A hundred more pupils, at least.

TOM: Your resources are great for a state / primary.

JO: You're an economist aren't you? You can see how that plays out.

TOM: Yeah, this is my school too. It's not a thought exercise, I'm part of it.

JO: My staff are working sixty-five hour weeks. Probably seventy. That's on top of marking, and lesson planning, that's their free time. And they come in when they're ill because no one can afford to miss an inspection. But the thing is, Tom, you take one session a week. And you can't show me a lesson plan.

TOM: I've tried to show you all year.

JO: You give the same service to all your clients?

Beat. TOM is wounded, JO is too exhausted to be exasperated, but she's close. TOM turns to LARA, who can't meet his gaze.

TOM: Ok. In my classes, we discuss things they've taken an interest in, that's what the songs and the videos are. But it's not a free ride, I'm challenging the way they think / about these –

JO: Tom. By the time they're in Year Seven every textbook they get – History, Maths, Science – expects them to be fluent readers. So will their teachers. You can't challenge the way they think until they have those skills.

TOM: But I'm engaging them, and if that's through music, or a film –

JO: Without those skills, they will be left behind. And that goes beyond school, we're talking about jobs, their health – if they can't read...

TOM: They can.

JO: No. No, some of them can't.

JO's mobile buzzes on the table. She goes to pick it up.

LARA: What do you mean?

JO: *(Answering her mobile.)* Hello?

TOM: Yeah, what does that mean?

JO: Hi, Sarah. Are you on your way back?

TOM: They can read, Jo. I've seen them.

JO holds her hand up, silencing him.

JO: Have you? I haven't –

She turns to her office phone. The light flashes.

JO: They should have been forwarded to me – ok, slow down.

She walks through the door, brushing past TOM, across LARA's office. TOM half follows.

JO: When? Just a second. *(To LARA.)* I have to take this.

LARA nods, JO exits into corridor and closes the door. TOM is stranded in LARA's office next to the sofa.

TOM: What was that?

LARA: Shut up, Tom.

TOM: I didn't know the parents were paying, no one ever bothered to / tell me.

LARA: It's not about that.

TOM: What is it about, then? I didn't dump her.

LARA: Careful.

LARA stands. As TOM speaks she goes into JO's office to the filing cabinets, searches through all three.

TOM: If she's got that much of a problem she could have told me ages ago. Lara, come on, that was not fair. I don't agree with grammar schools, nobody fucking does.

LARA finds the results, begins to open them.

TOM: And the education budget's been ring-fenced, y'know, protected. She treats me like I don't know what's happening. A whole chapter of my dissertation was on redistributing spending in education. It was pre-Brexit, but still, if you integrate with social services you can start on literacy before they start school –

LARA: Shit.

TOM: What?

LARA continues to read the letter.

TOM: What's that?

TOM enters JO's office and leans over LARA's shoulder to read it.

TOM: Are these the results?

LARA: One sec.

TOM scans them, holds an edge of the paper.

TOM: Hey, these are good!

LARA doesn't respond, running the numbers.

TOM: Jesus Christ, why's she kicking off?

LARA: They're not enough.

TOM: What do you mean?

LARA: To put in for the awards.

TOM: What awards?

LARA: The pupil premium awards. We haven't got a chance.

TOM: I thought it was just a grant system?

LARA: No, there's a prize scheme, and / it's –

TOM: Isn't everyone eligible?

LARA: You should only apply if eighty percent of pupils hit the national average. Or above. That's twenty-six kids.

TOM walks to LARA, takes the paper, checks it.

TOM: How many did we get?

LARA: Twenty-two.

TOM: So, what?

LARA: We can't apply.

TOM: We just can't go for the awards?

LARA: No.

TOM: Oh.

TOM checks the figures again.

TOM: You still get the premiums next year, don't you?

LARA: Yeah. At the current rate.

TOM: What do you mean?

LARA: It means less.

Beat. The fluorescent flickers.

TOM: Can we not still apply and see / what –

LARA: It has to be eighty percent.

TOM: Won't they take the higher scores into account?

LARA: Yeah, what about the lower ones?

TOM: We can put them in for a remark, they might go / up…

LARA: Look at those names. Those nine are nowhere near the average. They might get a couple of marks in a couple of papers.

TOM: Exactly.

LARA: But it won't change the grade, Tom. That's the point.

Silence.

TOM: You should get them remarked anyway.

LARA: They've already been moderated.

TOM: Those marks will mean a lot to them. And it only needs three to go up. That could definitely happen.

LARA: How did they do in your pre-assessment tests?

TOM: From the revision guides?

LARA: If that's what you used.

TOM: Above national average. I think.

LARA: In every paper?

TOM: Not every one.

LARA: *(Checking the results.)* Medha, Helena, Emily Rose, John Paul, Tom, Seb, Char, Rashid, –

TOM: Hannah.

LARA: – and Hannah.

TOM: Look, I know who they are.

LARA: The ones who needed the most help.

TOM: They were getting the scores… We were making progress.

LARA: Were you?

TOM: They've made progress. It's not my fault –

LARA: What's not?

TOM: They didn't turn up half the time.

Pause. A bell rings outside and the sounds of the playground fade. TOM is panicking.

TOM: She could've told me.

LARA: No. She needed this.

TOM: But I'm their teacher. How am I meant to teach them now?

LARA: She hasn't told the governors, she didn't tell me / and I was in –

TOM: You're just a secretary.

Half-beat.

LARA: Yeah. I suppose that's why.

TOM: And now I've got to stand there in front of them – she's made me look like a fucking idiot.

On the final word TOM punches the filing cabinet. He struggles to hide how much it hurt.

LARA: I think you should leave now. *(Beat.)* Can I have that please?

TOM hands over the results, crumpled in his hand. Murmurings of pupils filing into school fill the hallway. TOM leaves JO's office, picking up his rucksack and the Carluccio's bag from the sofa. At the door into the corridor he turns.

TOM: I'm coming back. You can tell her.

TOM exits. LARA folds the results, smoothes them out.

LARA: Fuck's sake.

She puts them back into the envelope on the table and replaces it in the filing cabinet. She turns to JO's desk, sees the receiver lying next to the phone. She replaces it, then plays the voicemail.

VOICEMAIL: Jo, it's Tony, just to let you know I've had a quick look at the fluoro and I've had to nip out for a new bulb –

She skips it. Next message:

VOICEMAIL: Me again, don't know if you got the last message or if you're coming tomorrow. You're going to have to let me know so we can rearrange if we have to. Unless you've changed your mind –

LARA hurriedly skips it. Next message:

VOICEMAIL: Jo, it's Sarah, I've tried you and Lara a few times but no one's picking up, I don't know if you've heard yet. You need call me back, I'm at St Margaret's General.

LARA walks out of JO's office and goes to her desk. She takes her phone out of the drawer and turns it on, lays it on her desk. It starts to vibrate. Missed calls.

JO enters from the corridor, still on the phone. She walks through to her office and picks up her bag.

JO: ...and you've called them both? No, I can get there...
Ok... Thanks, Sarah, I'll be with you in a bit. I'm sorry you couldn't get through. Ok.

JO hangs up.

JO: Why didn't you pick up?

LARA: You said to forward all calls to you.

JO: Yeah but, I was – Jesus.

LARA: Sarah called.

JO darts across LARA's office, into her own.

JO: I know.

JO roots through her bag, doesn't reply. LARA's phone vibrates on the desk again – more missed calls.

LARA: What's happened?

JO: It's fine. It's fine.

Beat. JO picks up the bloods kit, looks at it, then puts it in her bag.

LARA: I know that was Sarah, Jo. She's tried to call me seven times. *(Glancing at her phone.)* Eight.

JO begins to leave. LARA stops her.

LARA: Jo!

They stop.

JO: Hannah's been taken to hospital.

LARA's phone continues to vibrate in her hand.

End of Act 2.

Interstitial

TONY appears in the corridor again, looks up at the fluorescent light. He is holding a stepladder and a long strip bulb. He sets these down. He enters the office, changes the hands on both clocks to 3.10pm; he locks the door to JO's office as he exits to the corridor. He climbs the stepladder, takes the plastic casing off the light and begins to replace the bulb.

Act 3

Noises of the playground as pupils leave for the day. The bloods kit remains on JO's desk. The door of LARA's office is open, giving a view out on to the empty corridor.

Through the window we see TONY completing his task. He climbs down from the stepladder, moving out of sight in the window of the offices. Fast footsteps echo down the corridor; as TOM reaches the office he almost collides with TONY, who has turned around with the stepladder and broken bulb.

TONY: Mind it.

TOM: Sorry.

TONY doesn't respond, but walks past TOM down the corridor. TOM enters the office.

TOM: Jo?

He goes to JO's office door and knocks.

TOM: It's Tom. Can we have a chat?

A pause. He tries the handle with no luck.

TOM: Could you open the door? *(Half-beat.)* Please?

He waits. Then he closes the door to the corridor. He stands by JO's door, eventually sitting on LARA's desk.

TOM: You were going to let me go in there, and you already. *(Beat. Under his breath.)* You gave me this [job] –

JO enters from the corridor.

JO: Hi Tom.

Beat. LARA's office feels smaller than before.

TOM: Can we have a quick chat?

JO: I don't have time.

TOM: It won't take long.

JO: I'm in a bit of a rush.

TOM: Where have you got to be?

JO: None of your business.

TOM: Ok.

TOM nods. JO starts towards her office door.

JO: I need to get through, Tom.

TOM: I know you think I didn't try. But I did. And I went off course sometimes because I wanted them to enjoy it.

JO: We can talk about this –

TOM: It's the end of their day, I just wanted to give it – energy? I don't know. Because they hate the syllabus.

JO: I'm really just passing through. We can talk next week.

JO unlocks her office door and gathers her things from the desk. TOM talks at her as she goes to her filing cabinet, withdrawing Local Authority files and school liability insurance.

TOM: You never gave me any support. Or your teachers. Even little things, like no one ever asked if I wanted a tea in the staffroom. Never. And I know Miss Hopkins told Seb he could eat in my lessons, because, and I quote, 'it's not a proper lesson.' He told me that. In front of all of them. But I wanted them to do well.

JO sits at her desk and opens up the insurance document.

JO: I'm sure they will do.

TOM: I've seen the results, Jo.

JO: No you haven't.

TOM: When you left, earlier.

She faces him. He's not lying.

JO: You're not supposed to have seen those.

TOM: When were you going to tell me?

JO: Tell you what?

TOM: I know you didn't make the awards.

JO: How?

TOM: Lara told me.

Beat.

JO: I'll have a chat with her later. But I have a meeting in ten minutes, so I need you to / leave.

TOM: If my job was to get them ready for those exams, when were you going to tell me? I've screwed up your chances, for financial security / and you –

JO: Financial security?

TOM: Yeah for the prize, the award.

JO: It's not cash, Tom.

TOM: What?

JO: There's no money. Not since last year.

TOM: So... What's the problem?

JO: The awards are tickets, and workshops, and talks at galleries, museums, theatres. Conservatoires. Places they don't normally go. That's the problem.

TOM: I'm sorry –

JO: Don't be.

TOM: No, just – I thought they were cash.

JO: Used to be a hundred thousand pounds, yeah. Thank god you weren't here for that, you'd be really sorry then.

TOM: Jo, I get it –

JO: No you don't. If you know what a conservatoire is, you don't get it.

TOM: I agree the awards are important, / but –

JO: The awards are proof. That we're improving, that we're getting it right. But we didn't get it. You're kidding yourself if you thought we could. And what's the difference? They don't trust us with cash. At least on a school trip they can learn something new, right? Imagine if we were allowed to do that here.

TOM: You never told me I was here to help you.

JO: You weren't.

TOM: So Lara's kidding herself too?

JO: Imagine I'm not here at the moment. Ok? We can discuss /
this next week.

TOM: I can't teach them again.

JO: Again?

TOM: I can't do it.

JO: You have three more sessions. You're going to take them.

TOM: But now I know – don't make me.

JO: This is not about you.

TOM: Yeah, but it was my job / to –

JO: It doesn't matter.

TOM: How does it not matter?

JO: Because you haven't made a difference.

TOM: That matters! To me.

JO: You didn't bring them up. But you were never going to.
You didn't bring them down, though, so.

TOM: I could have brought them up.

JO: You're not qualified. You haven't trained. You've got a
nice degree but the fact that an agency's dropped you in
here doesn't make you a teacher. You didn't know the
curriculum had changed.

TOM: But you're talking just about scores – you can't tick a
box off for the entire learning process.

JO checks the clock on the wall.

JO: Alright, let me show you how this works.

*Calmly, efficiently, she consults her whiteboard, a reflection of TOM's
earlier demonstration, colder now. She circles or underlines the dates
with a pen.*

JO: Since you started here we've had three summative
assessments for Year Six.

TOM: Summative assessments?

JO: Mock SATs.

TOM: Say that, then.

JO: November, February, and April.

TOM: Ok.

JO: You knew about those.

TOM: You didn't tell me.

JO: I did. Let's run these numbers. *(She retrieves files from one of the cabinets.)* November: ten below, two above, the rest at national average – projected national average, whatever that means. February: eleven below, three above, sixteen on the average. And April: the same. So, consistent.

TOM: Four of them are well above that average.

JO: Who takes credit for that? Them? Their teachers? You?

TOM: Well, I didn't sit the exam.

JO: So there we are. You haven't made a difference either way.

TOM: But what I taught them –

JO: That's teaching, Tom. It's all the same, it's just the topics change. And you've got to tick the boxes.

TOM: So that's it, then?

JO: Look, if you want someone to blame it's the governors for deciding how to use the money.

TOM: So I blame you.

JO: I didn't vote for tutoring.

TOM: You're a governor.

JO: Yes, and I was overruled.

TOM: What would you have had?

JO: I don't know. iPads, more books, more staff. I wouldn't have brought in someone who makes rich kids richer.

TOM: Woah, that's – I don't do that.

JO: The biggest difference you've made is outside this school, where you tutor kids – who are already free readers – one on one. Getting them ready for admissions tests my pupils have no chance of taking. And you think it's not a proper job but it doesn't happen in a vacuum, Tom. You're just widening the gap.

TOM: So you were right. You can go back to the governors with your head held high. You won.

JO is exiting into the corridor, the door open.

JO: Yes, Tom, I wanted to sabotage my own school. I want my kids below national average.

TOM: They're not. They can write poems, and stories –

JO: What about in six months' time? Or two years from now?

TOM: – but that's not in your curriculum so it's worthless.

JO: *(Slamming the door.)* It's not my curriculum. You think we love it? You think I want them to be graded like this? Seven year olds? I have to suck it up, and so do you.

LARA's office phone rings. JO presses a button, sends it to voicemail.

JO: We teach them to succeed in the system because it's the system. Not because we want to. And it's the same system that takes away their school meals and doubles the amount of time they spend here. That tells me this place can be bought by sponsors whenever we are deemed to be failing. Because every school is failing until proven otherwise. That is the threat. *(Half-beat.)* That a company can do it better. If you want to teach those kinds of lessons, run a club. Or go back to your old school. This isn't the place.

TOM: If I'd known they were just numbers that's how I would have taught them.

JO: Numbers.

TOM: Data. So you could get your prize.

There is a strange pause.

JO: Why did you come back in here?

TOM: To talk to you.

JO: You could have gone home.

TOM: I didn't want to.

JO: I know why.

TOM: Do you?

JO: Same reason you arrived in the first place. For you. You thought it was enough to come in here and bless us with your presence. You are so wrapped up in your privileged little worldview that you really thought you could swan in here and produce a class of geniuses by doing whatever the hell you wanted. That's the world you've grown up in. Don't you dare deny it. You just haven't been caught out yet because your clients don't care what you do. It's enough that you're posh. And went to Winchester, then Oxford. You're an accessory. You're a little taster of the kind of person they want their spoiled brats to be. An elite teacher for the next generation of psychopaths. And you're not even that. Because when you go away, I bet they call you 'the help.' Don't kid yourself. You're a product. And you let that happen. You like the idea of teaching, maybe. But you're doing it because you have no idea what else to do, which is not enough, and you thought this would be a charity case. Do some good work on the wrong side of the tracks. The one time some pupils might have actually needed you, and you did nothing. They didn't need your background, they needed you. And you failed. And that's not the same as failing at your kind of school, or your kind of uni. They encourage failure because god knows you've got to taste it sometime, better now when it doesn't matter, try again next time. My kids don't get a next time. I can't afford to give them one. You saw what you had to do, you didn't like it, it wasn't interesting, it wasn't stimulating, it was below you. Because you didn't care what they had to learn, it was all about you.

TOM: We're not all the same.

JO: You all do the same thing, though.

TOM: That is not true.

JO: What then? You didn't try because you thought you *might* fail? And that's just not like you, is it, Tom? Double first from Oxford. Don't want any blemishes. So you went 'off-book,' like the maverick you are, a real rule-breaker. You jumped through every hoop they put in front of you, and just because that didn't make you the person you wanted to be, you tell my pupils to forget about it. That it doesn't matter. You pulled the ladder up. You took advantage of your position. You undermined my staff. Me. You held everything you had in front of them, all your learning, your intelligence, but you couldn't share it. Because you don't respect them, or where they come from. You snob. And the worst part of it is that they really like you. So yeah, you didn't fail, because you never tried. You've never seen failure.

TOM: I have, I –

JO: Have you seen a school close down?

TOM: What?

JO: Have you? And I don't mean 'have you read about it.'

TOM: No.

JO: I was nine. My first school. It was a convent school. Run by nuns. They were strict, but they weren't teachers. They'd beat us, with rulers. Sometimes a rod. Actual nuns. And I remember us shuffling around, never smiling. Saying Hail Marys to save the school. We weren't ten. Closed down because they couldn't get the numbers in the end.

And then I saw it again, seven years ago. St Michael's. But I saw the way it worked that time. The school was good, so the pupils came. Families moved to the area just so they could send their kids there. And of course the school couldn't keep up with demand, but we had to teach them. And then we had to try to teach them. Then some of us stopped trying. Teachers leave, good teachers, but the pupils keep flooding in. Because where else do you send them? And they get this look on their faces, the same one I know I had. Where you know something's happening, something beyond knowing the place is in special measures, but you can't say what it is. So they act out, start fights, stop working, you throw this on top of all the crap they're already dealing with. Because some of them are dealing with a lot. And I have to send them back to that. And when your school closes, how can you not feel like you're part of the problem? I wanted to tell them, shake it out of some of them, that it wasn't, wasn't them. Because I wanted someone to do that for me.

JO's not really talking to TOM.

JO: You do wonder if you give a shit anymore. It's never enough. There's no time. Everything we did last year, the improvement meetings, the reading curriculum, all that progress. *(Beat.)* Still I have to force eleven year olds to take exams, just so we can take care of them. They hold this prize over us like it's a favour. Like we need an incentive. When that award is the bare minimum this school should have. Every school should. And they wonder why we leave.

Pause. JO looks at the board.

JO: I want them to read. To be able to. No one even knows what the scores mean. And I don't really care about the scores. An academy might. Maybe an academy could do it better.

TOM: Do what better?

JO starts a little, aware of TOM in front of her.

JO: Teach.

TOM: Is that going to happen? *(Beat.)* Does Lara know?

JO: She doesn't need to. Does she?

TOM: No. *(Beat.)* They can read. And this can't be the way to boost morale. If this is how – if you talk like this to your colleagues, they must get pretty down.

JO looks at him and smiles. There is no malice.

JO: You're not a colleague, Tom. You're paid too much.

TOM: I'm gonna call TruThought. Get a replacement.

He exits. Silence in the room; faintly, the sounds of the playground.

JO sits, staring after him. She leans back in the chair, looks up at the ceiling. She sits forward, rubs her neck, then puts her fingers to the keyboard in front of her and begins to draft an email. After a while she stops. She takes the ibuprofen tablets still lying on the desk, puts them in her mouth. She searches for a cup on the table; there is none. She stands and walks through LARA's office, to the coffee station. All the mugs are dirty. She goes to exit into the corridor, stops. She returns to her office, pulls a plastic bottle out of her bag. It is empty.

She throws the bottle into the wastepaper basket at her feet. She swallows the pills dry, then sits at the desk. Suddenly she hits the keyboard with the palm of her hand, very hard, once. She stops herself from repeating the action, sits still.

She presses a button on the phone. A beep.

VOICEMAIL: Hello, only me. I can't get through on the mobile so I thought I'd try you here, you must, um – not be in yet. I know it's not ideal, but you're not picking up at home either, so… Yep. Just checking you were all set for tomorrow, might be nice to talk to you without the solicitor. I found the marriage certificate, so you can stop looking for that. If you were looking. I'll try again later. And they said it wouldn't take long, so if you want maybe we could get a coffee afterwards. Anyway, give me a call when you get this. Be good to hear your voice before it's official. Hope all's ok at work. *(Beat.)* We are going to have to talk at some stage. Ok. Bye, Jo.

A beep. JO stares into space, then goes to the plant pot and begins to water the plants.

She is distracted by the flickering fluorescent. She stands, and is drawn towards it. She is in front of the board. Her eyes lower from the strip window to the board in front of her. She scans it, steps back a little.

The phone vibrates on the desk. She turns her head slightly; the sounds of the playground begin to rise. Then she takes the wipe-board spray and the cloth from the shelf that runs beneath the board. She sprays and erases the dinosaur doodle and watches the empty space.

The phone vibrates again. The fluorescent flickers. The playground is growing to a deafening crescendo. With the spray and the cloth in hand, JO cleans the whiteboard, as long as it takes until it is spotless, growing more frantic as the noise of the playground builds and the fluorescent grows brighter... and brighter... and brighter.

JO: Shut up. Shut up, just, just for a minute... Please shut up, PLEASE.

The light returns to normal. The sounds of the playground return to a soft murmur, a bell rings softly. The fluorescent's steady glow is interrupted by a couple of flickers.

JO breathes softly. There are raised voices in the corridor followed by a pair of footsteps. JO replaces the watering can.

DAVID Martin, Hannah's father, enters from the corridor. He is around JO's age and has come straight from work. He looks towards JO's office and moves into it. LARA follows him, speaking from offstage and continuing onstage. She is playing with her glasses. TOM is trapped in JO's doorway.

LARA: Please, if you just wait in the main office I'll see if she's free –

DAVID: Where's Hannah?

LARA: *(To DAVID.)* Mr Martin, if you just wait in my office –

DAVID: I've been told to meet her here.

LARA: Jo, I can call the / police –

JO: It's fine Lara, we arranged to –

DAVID: Where's Hannah?

JO: She's at the hospital, David.

DAVID: Why wasn't I called?

JO: We tried you from there, but we couldn't get through.

DAVID: I've been at work.

JO: That explains it, then.

DAVID: So, what, they didn't bring her back here then?

JO: No. We arranged to meet here so I could explain – Hannah's mum asked.

DAVID: Why can't she tell me herself?

JO: Because she's at the hospital.

DAVID: Where am I meant to pick her up from?

JO: She's staying. Overnight.

DAVID: Which one?

JO: St Margaret's.

DAVID: Why do they need to keep her?

JO: She had a hypoglycaemic fit.

Beat.

DAVID: On this trip?

JO: Yes.

DAVID: I told you she wasn't well.

JO: Mr Martin, I didn't force her to–

DAVID: You rang me up asking me where she was.

JO: Because you hadn't contacted the school.

DAVID: She didn't want to go.

JO: I don't think that's true, David. When I spoke to her –

DAVID: It doesn't matter what she said to you.

TOM enters, putting his phone into his pocket.

JO: David, I only let her go once you told me her bloods were fine.

DAVID: So this is my fault?

JO: No, but if you had / taken them –

DAVID: What are you saying, you saying I'm lying?

JO: If her bloods were fine this shouldn't have happened. The only reason we didn't check them is because you said you'd already taken them.

DAVID: I told you I don't have a bloods kit.

JO: You said you bought one. This morning. That's why you were late.

Half-beat.

DAVID: Yeah, that's why I bought one.

JO: Do you have it with you?

DAVID: I gave it to her.

JO: But – I just don't think this would have happened if she'd had a kit.

DAVID: Why not?

JO: Because she understands her diabetes.

DAVID: Oh, come on.

JO: It's not a dirty word.

DAVID: I know, yeah, I know.

JO: Did you take her bloods?

Beat.

JO: Did she have a kit?

DAVID: It's your job to provide one for her.

JO: The school has one, and I still have hers here. I don't teach classes anymore, Mr Martin, so I don't get the chance to look after many pupils, but I've / taken [an exception].

DAVID: What? You've got two hundred of them.

JO: What I mean is, if I have a student, like Hannah, who is going through a hard time –

DAVID: What's that supposed to mean?

JO: It means that she's diabetic, and I'm not sure she's getting adequate attention / [when she's at home].

DAVID: Hang on – I didn't sign a permission slip.

JO: Sorry?

DAVID: For the trip. I never signed one.

JO: I gave you one, I took it back here.

DAVID: No, you didn't.

JO: Lara, check the file, please.

LARA retrieves the file with the cheques and permission slips, alphabetically filed.

DAVID: You can check all you want, I didn't sign anything.

JO: No child was allowed on the bus without one, it's school policy. Lara?

LARA: I'm just checking... I've got a cheque but no slip.

DAVID: Yeah, that's from her mum. She didn't sign one either, then?

JO: You're checking under 'Martin?'

LARA: Yeah.

JO: Check under 'H.'

LARA: *(Flicking back.)* I did it by surname... It's not here.

DAVID: And you're blaming me.

JO: I didn't blame you –

DAVID: When it's your responsibility.

JO: You were late, the bus was about to – I apologize, I thought I gave you one but I must / have –

DAVID: So I didn't give my permission.

JO: We sent out permission slips a month ago.

DAVID: I told you, I never got one.

JO: Then it must have gone to – to Hannah's mum. She signed the cheque.

DAVID: We've separated.

Half-beat.

JO: Well, if you give my assistant your new address we can put you on the system so this doesn't happen again. I appreciate how stressful this must all be.

LARA: Mr Martin, I can take it down now. Or you can write it here if you like.

DAVID: *(To JO, with building aggression.)* No, sorry, I'm not having this. You don't question me. This happened while she was under your care. You forced her to go and look what happened. Not your job, is it? I said no, and that makes you liable. And how long has she been in hospital and I didn't even know? *(Gesturing to TOM and LARA.)* How long have they known? And I didn't? *(Beat.)* You had no right to make her go. She's not yours. If you had kids of your own, you'd have known to leave it. It's a fucking hard job, and I don't need anyone else sticking their nose in. You think it helps when everyone's watching you, waiting for your big fucking mistake? And I don't appreciate you talking down at me when you can't keep your divorce out of the playground.

Beat.

JO: I don't think that's relevant to how I run this school.

DAVID: We'll see what your governors think. Since you took over, I don't like what's happening here. I'll let them know that as well.

DAVID exits. TOM, JO and LARA stand fixed in place. Footsteps echo away, fall to silence.

LARA: *(Eventually, faltering.)* Jo, I tried to stop him.

Pause. JO goes to her handbag, pulls out a crumpled permission slip, nods. She smoothens it on her desk, then looks at the liability insurance.

JO: I thought I'd given it to him.

LARA: I should have noticed.

JO: No, no. *(Beat.)* He didn't ask if she was ok.

LARA: Is she?

JO: She's fast asleep. They're keeping her under observation, should be out tomorrow.

LARA: What was it?

JO: Seizure. Her blood sugars were through the floor.

LARA: It happened at the museum?

JO: Just before lunch. Ten minutes away from a sandwich and a cookie. Might have done the trick. Ten minutes. *(Gathers herself.)* I mean it's happened before. This was more severe, I think, the rush this morning... Paramedics got there really quickly, museum staff knew what to do. Sarah was brilliant, apparently.

LARA: Is she going to be ok?

JO: They said it's a miracle she didn't crack her head on the – because it's all marble... *(Beat.)* I know he didn't take her bloods.

LARA: I know.

JO: And we had slack for two absent, didn't we?

LARA nods.

JO: So she could have missed it.

LARA doesn't respond.

JO: She looked so small.

LARA is silent. TOM watches JO intently.

JO: I made her go.

LARA: Of course you did.

Beat.

LARA: I cancelled the staff meeting.

JO: Thanks.

LARA: And I let them know. I hope that's ok.

JO: That's ok.

LARA: And I can tell them – she's alright? Now?

JO: We'll have to wait 'til tomorrow.

LARA: None of the kids know.

JO: They've got Snapchat. They all know. *(Beat.)* I'm going back to the hospital, if you're ok here?

LARA: Are you sure?

JO: I have to.

TOM: This is Year Six Hannah?

JO: Yeah.

TOM: She's diabetic?

LARA nods.

TOM: Fuck.

JO: Yeah.

Beat.

TOM: I'm so sorry.

JO: You didn't know.

TOM: Jo, that wasn't fair. That was… What a fucking prick.

JO: It's ok.

TOM: Yeah but I'm – you're going back to the hospital? I'll drive you.

JO: Tom, you have a lesson, so what I need you to do now –

TOM: We'll cancel it. Fuck the agency if they can't get a replacement.

JO: The pupils won't get picked up.

TOM: I want to help. Please.

JO: You can't. You have to stop thinking you can. This was was my fault. If you feel bad about it –

TOM: I *do* feel bad.

JO: – hide it.

TOM: I can't –

JO: Tom, you're acting like –

TOM: Like what?

JO: Like a bloody [child].

MIKAELA, a pupil aged ten, appears in the office. She is carrying her school rucksack over one shoulder. A beat.

LARA: Hello Mikaela.

MIKAELA: Hello.

LARA: Oh, yeah. Mummy's going to be a bit late today isn't she?

MIKAELA nods.

MIKAELA: Miss Hopkins told me to come here.

LARA: Ok, well you can sit on the sofa 'til mummy comes.

MIKAELA sits on the sofa. JO turns, defeated by one more tiny problem, towards her office. LARA follows to the threshold. TOM begins to follow, then turns and whips his phone out of his pocket. He hands it to MIKAELA.

TOM: Have you ever played Pokémon Go?

MIKAELA: Yeah.

TOM: Great. Don't delete anything, ok?

MIKAELA: Ok.

TOM turns back to the doorway between the offices. Keeping their voices down:

JO: I'm leaving now, Tom.

TOM: What am I –

JO: Take the lesson.

TOM: I'm not a teacher.

LARA: I'll do it. *(Beat.)* I know all the kids in that class. And the syllabus. I can do it.

TOM: Is that…?

JO: Who's going to stay with Mikaela?

LARA: Tom can.

TOM: Yeah, that's fine.

JO: Lara, you haven't taught a class before.

LARA: You said I could train here.

JO: What about your dad?

LARA: What about him?

JO: Don't you need to get home?

LARA: I'll call, he'll understand.

JO: You're sure?

LARA: I'll ask the nurse to stay a bit longer.

JO: Can you do that?

LARA: I've done it before.

JO: Ok. *(Beat.)* He wouldn't have let this happen.

LARA: Jo. I've got this, you should go.

JO: Alright. Alright. *(Beat.)* Don't tell him?

LARA: I won't.

JO: It's not his school.

JO opens the door.

JO: Goodbye Mikaela.

MIKAELA: Bye Miss Fell.

TOM: Send my best to Hannah.

JO: I will.

LARA suddenly remembers something.

LARA: Jo.

She dashes to JO's desk and picks up the bloods kit. She gives it to JO.

LARA: See you tomorrow.

JO: You'll be great.

LARA: *(Grabbing a book off the desk.)* And the next Biff, Chip and Kipper. Carolyn left it for you. Year 3 didn't want you to fall behind.

JO: *(Taking the book.)* No. Wouldn't want that. *(Beat.)* Did the attendance reports come through?

LARA: Still waiting.

JO: I'll get onto that tomorrow.

JO exits. LARA begins collecting folders from her desk drawer, flipping through until she finds a suitable KS2 lesson plan. TOM realizes something.

LARA: Mikaela's mum is going to be here at 3.45, is that alright?

TOM: You're going back to the PGCE.

LARA: I'm applying.

TOM: But you've done it before?

LARA: I dropped out.

TOM: If I'd known I wouldn't have – I would have shut up.

LARA: Look, Mikaela's mum is going to be here at three forty-five, is that alright?

TOM: 'Course, yeah. I'll make sure you get paid for today. I'll speak to the agency.

LARA: If you want.

TOM: Do you want to take the rest of the sessions?

LARA: One step at a time, Tom.

TOM: Ok. Just, don't use TruThought? They don't give a shit.

MIKAELA: *(Gasping.)* He swore.

LARA: Tom.

TOM: Sorry, Mikaela. *(To LARA.)* You should take the lessons.

LARA: *(Stacking the materials on her desk.)* Mikaela, you're going to wait here with Mr Rawlence, ok?

MIKAELA: Ok.

TOM: Do you want my lesson plan?

LARA: I'll just work with mine. Just need to get these worksheets photocopied.

TOM: Ok.

LARA: Ok.

LARA exits with her worksheets. TOM stands in the middle of the office, sits on LARA's desk. The sounds of a classroom gather outside: Year Six are back.

MIKAELA: Are you a teacher?

Beat.

TOM: Um. I teach Year Six sometimes.

MIKAELA: You don't look like a teacher.

TOM: Why's that?

MIKAELA: No tie.

TOM: Miss Fell doesn't wear a tie.

MIKAELA: Because she's the headteacher. She's in charge, so she doesn't have to.

TOM: True.

MIKAELA: She could if she wanted to though.

(Beat.)

TOM: So, how are you, Mikaela?

MIKAELA: Fine.

TOM: Did you have a good day at school?

MIKAELA: I'm still at school.

TOM: Fair enough. What are you going to do when you get home?

MIKAELA: I'm going gardening with my dad.

TOM: In your garden, or...?

MIKAELA: We don't have a garden.

TOM: Oh. So how are you going to go gardening?

MIKAELA: It's his job.

TOM: Your dad's a gardener? That's a wicked job!

MIKAELA: Yeah.

TOM: Does he work for the council?

MIKAELA: I don't know, maybe.

TOM: Well, where does he go gardening?

MIKAELA: Loads of different places.

TOM: Do you think you might want to be a gardener when you grow up?

MIKAELA: *(Considers.)* Maybe. But I want to do the proper gardening, it's boring now.

TOM: I bet it's not.

MIKAELA: How do you know?

TOM: Because… I garden sometimes. You can do weeding, or put flowers in the ground.

MIKAELA: I've never done that.

TOM: Maybe when you're a bit older, then. Your dad has to make sure everything's done properly, all the lawns and hedges.

MIKAELA: But all I get to do is knock at the door and talk to the people.

TOM: What do you mean?

MIKAELA: I knock at the door and ask if the people need a gardener.

TOM: So you and dad ask people if they need gardening done?

MIKAELA: No, just me, because when I ask the people he goes around the house to look at their garden.

TOM: Oh. Ok. *(Beat.)* Why does he do that?

MIKAELA: Because he says sometimes people say they don't need a gardener when actually they do.

TOM: So while you talk to the person… He's 'round the back of the house…?

MIKAELA: Yeah. He does an inspection.

TOM: Oh. Do you go gardening near where you live, Mikaela?

MIKE: No, we go far away, like miles away, and then we come back very late. But I only go once a week, so it's fine.

TOM: So your dad's a gardener.

MIKAELA: Yeah. Someone gave him a TV once.

A pause. The noise of the nearby classroom has grown. Footsteps down the corridor. LARA enters.

LARA: Ok, I'm going to have to lock the office up.

TOM: Oh, yeah. Shall we wait in the playground?

LARA: Yeah, if that's ok. Mikaela, mummy's going to be here in ten minutes, so Mr Rawlence will wait with you until she arrives.

MIKAELA: Ok. *(To TOM.)* Can I keep playing?

TOM: Yeah, just watch where you're going.

MIKAELA wanders slowly towards the door, waiting in the doorway. TOM turns to LARA, who is putting the sheets into a folder. He speaks quietly.

TOM: Uh, has she spoken about her dad before?

LARA: The gardener?

TOM: Yeah.

LARA: Yeah.

TOM: And you all –

LARA: Yeah.

TOM: But you can't –

LARA: No.

Beat. There's nothing either of them can do.

TOM: What are you going to say about Hannah?

LARA: That she's ok.

TOM: I didn't know. I don't know anything.

LARA: You know some things.

TOM: Good luck.

LARA: Thanks.

TOM: And don't forget to call your dad.

LARA: Oh, yeah. Thanks, Tom.

LARA takes out her phone. As she dials, TOM goes towards the door where MIKAELA is waiting. He takes his school lanyard from around his neck and leaves it on the desk.

TOM: Come on, Mikaela.

TOM exits with MIKAELA, still talking. As TOM and MIKAELA exit:

TOM: Hey, did you know velociraptors had feathers?

Their voices recede. The noise of the nearby classroom has grown further, rowdy, impatient now. LARA puts her phone in her bag and her glasses on. She picks up the pile of folders and sheets and tucks it under her arm. With her free hand she picks up her keys. She looks towards the door leading onto the corridor, inhales, and walks towards it. She leaves.

Blackout.

Silence.

The fluoro flickers once, then goes out.

End.

Printed in the USA
CPSIA information can be obtained
at www.ICGtesting.com
LVHW020859171024
794056LV00002B/613